Helion & Company Limited
Unit 8 Amherst Business Centre
Budbrooke Road
Warwick
CV34 5WE
England
Tel. 01926 499 619
Email: info@helion.co.uk
Website: www.helion.co.uk
Twitter: @helionbooks
Visit our blog http://blog.helion.co.uk/

Cover image: On 16 August 1964, six
    pilots of Republic RF-84F Thunderflash
    reconnaissance fighters of the Royal
    Hellenic Air Force, were tasked with
    flying photo-reconnaissance over
    Cyprus. One of the jets in question is
    visible in the foreground. Upon reaching
    the island, they were intercepted
    by English Electric Lighting F.Mk 3
    interceptors of No. 111 Squadron, Royal
    Air Force, one of which is visible in the
    background. Careful manoeuvring by
    British pilots successfully frustrated most
    of the Greek attempts to photograph
    their targets: only one RF-84F returned
    with images that were clear enough to
    interpret. (Artwork by Pablo Albornoz ©
    Helion & Company 2023)

Designed and typeset by Mach 3 Solutions
    (www.mach3solutions.co.uk)
Cover design Paul Hewitt, Battlefield Design
    (www.battlefield-design.co.uk)

ISBN 978-1-804512-12-8

British Library Cataloguing-in-Publication
    Data
A catalogue record for this book is available
    from the British Library

We always welcome receiving book
proposals from prospective authors.

CONTENTS

MAP OF EUROPE SINCE 1992

Note: In order to simplify the use of this book, all names, locations and geographic designations are as provided in *The Times World Atlas*, or other traditionally accepted major sources of reference, as of the time of described events.

ABBREVIATIONS

AB	air base
APC	armoured personnel carrier
CIA	Central Intelligence Agency (USA)
CO	Commanding Officer
COIN	counterinsurgency
CUP	Committee of Union & Progress (political movement in the late Ottoman Empire, partially reformed as the GNA in 1919–1922)
DP	Democratic Party (Turkey)
EAM	*Ethniko Apeleftherotiko Metopo*, National Liberation Front (leftist political party in Greece, 1941–1945)
EDES	*Ethnikos Dimokratikos Ellinikos Syndesmos*, National Republican Greek League (liberal and right-wing guerrilla movement in Greece, 1941–1945)
ELAS	*Ellinikos Laikos Apeleftherotikos Stratos* (military wing of the EAM, 1941–1945)
ELDYK	*Elliniki Dynami Kyprou* (Greek Cyprus Force; regiment-sized contingent of Greek Army deployed on Cyprus since 1960 with the purpose of training the Cypriot National Guard)
EOEA	*Ethnikes Omades Ellinon Antarton*, National Groups of Greek Guerrillas (transformation of EDES after 1943; also known as EDES-EOEA)
EOK	*Ethinki Organosi Kyprou* (Cyprus National Organisation; secret militia of Greek Cypriot government in 1963–1964, also known as 'Akritas Organisation')
EOKA	*Ethniki Organosis Kyprion Agoniston* (National Organisation of Cypriot Fighters or Struggle)
EVA	*Elliniki Vasiliki Aeroporia* (Royal Hellenic Air Force, 1934–1974)

EYP	*Ethiki Ypiresia Piroforion* (National Intelligence Agency; Greece)
GNA	*Grand National Assembly* (political movement then political party in the Ottoman Empire/Turkey of 1919–1922; reorganised as the RPP in 1923–1924)
HVKK	*Hava Kuvvetleri Komutanligi* ([Turkish] Air Force; in more recent times, TurAF is in widespread use in official documentation)
IDEA	*Ieros Desmos Ellinon Axiomatikon* ('Holy Bond', right-wing militant society of Greece, 1950s and 1960s)
KKE	*Kommounistiko Komma Elladas* (Communist Party of Greece)
KTKA	*Kibrus Türk Kuvvetleri Alayı* (Turkish Treaty Regiment: regiment-sized contingent of Turkish Land Forces on Cyprus since 1960 with the purpose of training the Cypriot armed forces)
MBT	main battle tank
PA	*Polemiki Aeroporia* (Hellenic Air Force; official designation in periods 1931–1934 and since 1974)
RPP	Republican People's Party (Turkey)
RHAF	Royal Hellenic Air Force (official designation from 1934 until 1974)
SAR	search and rescue
TDK	*Türk Deniz Kuvvetleri* (Turkish Naval Forces)
TKK	*Türk Kara Kuvvetleri* (Turkish Land Forces/Army)
TMT	*Türk Mukavemet Teskilati* (Turkish Resistance Organisation, Cyprus)
TRNC	Turkish Republic of Northern Cyprus
TSK	*Türk Silahli Kuvvetleri* (Turkish Armed Forces)
UNFICYP	United Nations Peacekeeping Force in Cyprus

NOTE

To simplify the use of this book, all names, locations and geographic designations are as provided in *The Times World Atlas*, or other traditional accepted major sources of reference, as of the time of the described events. When mentioned for the first time in the text, aircraft and heavy weapons system designations are cited fully – including their designer and/or the manufacturer, official military designation and nickname: in the case of Soviet-made armament: this is followed by the ASCC/NATO-reporting name, which is then used through the text.

PREFACE

The 'Cyprus Crisis' – also known as the 'Cyprus problem', 'Cyprus dispute', 'Cyprus issue', 'Cyprus question' or the 'Cyprus conflict' – is an ongoing dispute between the leaders of the Greek Cypriot community and that of the Turkish Cypriot community. It is a widely discussed and published topic, repeatedly hitting the headlines and capturing public attention for decades: however, when it comes to its military history written in the English language, the dispute is an under-published topic.

Although the animosity between Greece and Turkey dates back to the Greek struggle for independence from the Ottoman Empire, in the nineteenth century and the Turkish War of Independence of 1919–1922, the Greek and Turkish communities had previously lived together on Cyprus for centuries without serious strife. The situation only began to change once the island came under British control in 1878, but particularly once the Greek community began to agitate for *enosis* (union with Greece), in the 1950s. While the British sought for the way to get rid of the problem in 'honourable fashion', Greece and Turkey became directly involved. A 'solution' – of a rather temporary nature, as it turned out – was found in the form of the Zürich-London Agreements, which established an independent Cyprus based on the concepts of administrative separation of the two communities, even without their geographic separation. Foremost, for the agreements to work, they included Great Britain, Greece and Turkey who were able to intervene jointly or individually, in the internal affairs of the new state.

It was not only the lack of mutual trust, but the amount of extremism and opportunism on both sides that soon made a cooperative governance impossible – even more so because the Greek Cypriot majority of the population were determined to get rid of the constitutional provisions that gave the Turkish minority a veto power in matters of foreign affairs, defence, and key domestic issues. In turn, the Turkish Cypriots clung rigidly to the constitutional safeguards as their best protection against the Greek majority. The dispute came to a head in 1963, when the presidency of Cyprus attempted to amend the constitution in an attempt to create a unitary state under majority rule. In an already tense atmosphere, a 'minor' incident then sparked violence that rapidly spread over the island and almost caused a war between Greece and Turkey.

The work on this project actually began nearly 30 years ago, in the course of several online discussions related to the claims and counter-claims about air combats between aircraft of the Greek and Turkish air forces of 1974. Before soon, it became obvious that operations of both air forces were much more comprehensive than usually reported in the mainstream media: indeed, they included dozens of aircraft. Further research then led to the realisation that the crisis was not limited to 1974 but could be dated by events at least 10 years earlier. Over the years, collections of related books and articles became a profession, rather than hobby. Still, *Ripped Apart* is not meant to help anybody come to grips with Cyprus or explain who is right or wrong: we went as far as to point at who did what for the purpose of explaining the background and context for aerial operations which never take place spontaneously entirely on their own. We also became interested in explaining how this crisis came into being and what factors influenced its flow and then, as far as possible, record the military conflict and recollections of participants.

All three of us are passionate about military history and at least two of us are particularly passionate about military aviation. Correspondingly, we put special emphasis on this aspect of the Cyprus Crisis. However, as usual, in all the volumes of the @War book series, we went to some lengths to cover not only the military, but also historical and geographical backgrounds along with the involvement of both ground and naval forces. Not only because Greece and Turkey have equally fascinating and proud military histories (which are exercising influence upon the doctrine of their armed forces up to this very day), but especially because Greece and Turkey played a crucial role in the Cyprus Crisis. Their decisions were largely influenced by traumatic experiences from multiple wars of the nineteenth century and the first half of the twentieth century. Therefore, a large part of this volume is dedicated to a review of the geostrategic positions of Greece and Turkey and provides at least a superficial summary of some of the most important moments in their military history.

The book spends time discussing their military build-ups of the 1950s and 1960s and the topics in question are comprehensive to the extent that it is only in the second half of this book that we have found the space for tracing the political and military history of Cyprus up to the 1950s and especially, during the 1960s, along with other factors which affected this conflict. It also addresses the local military build-up and then an entire series of armed clashes that shook the island of 1964. The result being a book that is foremost, an introduction to the topic.

In the course of our work, we have adopted a judicious approach to detail, condensing some of the political developments – although understanding that this is certain to be analysed as 'bias' and 'prejudice'. We have decided to pursue a similar approach in regards to terminology: as in the case of many other conflicts of similar nature, the phraseology appears to be 'easily betraying one's standpoints' in regards to the Cyprus Crisis. Actually, we are following a pragmatic approach of adopting the standard usage of terms without any prejudice. For example, many of geographic locations have both Greek and Turkish names, and these are equally accepted in the wider public. For the reader's easier orientation, we have opted to use those usually accepted in English. Additionally, as this book is not meant to be a lecture in Greek or Turkish languages, we have decided to make use of geographic designations depending on who was the party in control at the given point in time. For example, we refer to Constantinople until the city was overrun by the Ottomans, and Istanbul afterwards, even though the official re-naming took place only in the 1920s. We use Turkey, although the official name of the country was meanwhile changed to Türkiye, as at the time of the events in question, it was still named Turkey. For similar reasons, we use Lefkosia, although Turkish Cypriots prefer Lefkoşa; Kyrenia although Girne is used by Turkish Cypriots and Paphos for what is known as Baf, to the Turkish Cypriots.

For the same reasons, when describing the Turkish military operation on Cyprus of 1974, we use the term 'intervention' (preferred by Turkish Cypriots) – not because we are aiming to take sides, but as in a military sense, the enterprise in question had the characteristics of an intervention, rather than any kind of an 'invasion' or 'peace operation', as insisted by many.

A project of this kind is never run by authors alone: rather a matter of collective work by many people, to whom we would like to express our gratitude. The staff of the National Archives, British Library, National Library of Scotland and different museums in Cyprus and Türkiye, have provided extensive help to Dave Watson over the time. We would like to thank them and to the veterans of the Turkish Armed Forces for their kind assistance and – in the latter case – the time to be interviewed. Dimitri Mitsainas, son of Major-General Georgios Mitsanas (author of the first comprehensive work on the operations of the Hellenic Air Force over Cyprus) has generously granted permission to Dimitris Vassilopoulos for the use of whatever parts of his father's book – something that might become obvious from quoted sources of reference. Ioannis Kakolyris, a former engineer of the Hellenic Air Force and pilot of the Olympic Airlines, veteran of the events of 1964–1974 and author of three books about this subject, has provided his similar permission, but also precious additional knowledge and insights. Something similar is valid for Ole Niklajsen and Dr. David Nicolle, who selflessly shared their immense knowledge about the Ottoman and Turkish Air Forces and the operations of the latter during the Cyprus Crisis. Another person strongly influencing our work was one of first Greek pilots of McDonnell-Douglas F-4 Phantom II, Lieutenant-General Panagiotis Bales, who provided extensive interviews and excerpts from his memoirs. Similar is valid for late Brigadier-General Kostas Dimitroulopoulos, who flew Northrop F-5A Freedom Fighters during the Second Cyprus Crisis of 1967 and recorded his recollections in the book 'In the Heights of Fighter Aircraft', the publishers of which kindly provided permission to use several excerpts for this project. Kyriakos Paloulian and Savvas Vlassis kindly granted permission of use of their excellent research about the mission of North American T-6 Harvards in Cyprus of 1964 and to use materials from interviews with various pilots, while Themis Vranas put us in touch with Brigadier-General Antonis Konstantakos who flew with the Cypriot Air Wing of the 1960s: it was a very special opportunity and a honour to interview him and it is hard to express all the gratitude for the information he has shared. We would also like to thank George Lambrakis who contributed with his excellent research regarding the F-84F operations during 1974 and the Turkish researcher, Levent Basara, who was eager all this time to help us and answer our questions regarding HVKK.

An insight of RHAF operations was also provided by former veteran pilots who served during the Cyprus Crisis, especially in 1974: Stylianos Petroulakis, Dionysios Kouris, Spiros Karahalios (and his nephew Alexis who brought us in contact). Last but not least, Sergios Papasis – one of the veteran Republic RF-84F Thunderflash-pilots who flew an operational sortie over Cyprus in August 1964 – and his colleague who kindly provided details on four of jets involved in that mission. Webmasters of the outstanding website htttps://www.thunderstreaks.com - Frank Klaasen and Johan A 'Hans' Engels, Themis and Nikolaos Trakas, Paschalis Palavouzis, John Terniotis, Kyriakos Paloulian, Spiros Karahalios, Panagiotis Mpales, Thanasis Hatzelakos, Dimitris Boudouris, Alexandros Megas, Ioannis Mylonas, John Ioannou and Hellenic Air Force History Museum who have helped with photographic materials, John Korellis contributed with his technical knowledge and photo interpretation on RHAF aircraft between 1940 to 50, especially on the T-6 story, as well as Andrew Phedonos who kindly visited Kew in London and provided us the Operational Record Book for 111 Squadron. We most sincerely hope that this book is going to live up to their expectations and that of so many other readers.

1

BACKGROUND

Much of Cyprus' history is related to that of Greece and Turkey: indeed, the fate of the island over the last 60 years was not only closely associated with these two cultures, but directly influenced by the politicians and politics of successive governments in Ankara and Athens. Unsurprisingly, both the forces of Greece and Turkey became directly involved on Cyprus, and thus any study of military history of related developments requires at least a superficial review of the local geography, history and a military build-up of both Greece and Turkey of the twentieth century.[1]

Terrain, Climate and Vegetation
Regarding military history, there is no denying that Greece and Turkey – or the powers controlling them – dominated the central and north-eastern Mediterranean: indeed, Turkey in particular, has a strategic position as a link between Europe and the Middle East.

Greece is positioned on a mountainous, southern tip of the Balkan Peninsula and includes two smaller peninsulas that project out from it: the Chalkidiki and the Peloponnese. The dominant mountain range across the centre of the country is the Pindus, stretching in a northwest-to-southeast direction, with a maximum elevation of 2,637m. The highest point is Mount Olympus, rising to 2,917m above sea level. Extensions of the Pindus range stretch across the Peloponnese and underwater across the Aegean Sea, forming many islands and archipelagos, from Moudros in the north, to Lesbos, Evia

and the Cyclades to Crete in the southern direction and from Rhodes and Karpathos to Crete in the western direction. The coastline totals around 13,700km (8,500 miles), making it one of the longest in the world: the coastal waters are shallow and characterised by plentiful gulfs and bays. Perhaps the best example are the gulfs of Corinth and Saronikos, separated by the Isthmus of Corinth, dividing the Peloponnese from central and northern Greece.

Plains are relatively few and mostly found in Thessaly, in the western Peloponnese, in central Macedonia and in western Thrace, while the Rhodope Mountains, along the border between Greece and Bulgaria, is covered by vast, thick forests. Local rivers are relatively short and mostly dry in the summer. Although the long northern border of modern-day Greece is largely mountainous, the corridors and natural communication lines are generally perpendicular to it and thus the mountain ranges do not form an effective barrier to invasions. This is compounded by the narrowness of the north-eastern part of the country – as was well-exposed both during the First and the Second World Wars.

To the east of this area is the Anatolian Peninsula, positioned in between the Black Sea in the north, the Sea of Marmara and the Aegean Sea in the West, and the Mediterranean Sea in the south. Nowadays, within the borders of Türkiye, geographically, this is divided into distinct regions: eastern Thrace, the Black Sea region; western Anatolia; the central Anatolian Plateau; the eastern highlands, south-eastern Anatolia, and the Aegean and Mediterranean regions. Eastern Thrace and the coast along the Sea of Marmara is a fertile, well-watered area containing a central plain of gently rolling hills, but the eastern portion of this region rises as high as 2,543m (8,343ft) atop Mount Ulu. The Cilician Gates through the Taurus Mountains connect the Çukurova plain in the interior, while the Anatolian coastlands of the Black Sea rise directly from the water to the heights of the Northern Anatolian Mountains, with very little arable land. Western Anatolia consists of irregular ranges and valleys where farming remains limited. Slightly more arable land can be found in the central Anatolian Plateau, the largest geographic region of Turkey; this is surrounded by mountains, the highest of which is Mount Erciyes at 3,916m (12,848ft). The eastern highlands is the most mountainous and rugged portion; dominated by Mount Ararat at 5,165m (16,945ft), this is the source of both the Tigris and Euphrates rivers. South-eastern Anatolia is another plateau enclosed by mountains and a part of the so-called 'Fertile Crescent' which has been highly important for human development since antiquity. The coastal lands of the Aegean and Mediterranean region are narrow and hilly and less than a fifth of the local land is arable. Almost all the rivers in Turkey contain rapids and many do not flow during the summer. While unsuitable for navigation, they are important sources of water for irrigation and hydroelectric power. At 1,150km (715 miles), the Kizilirmak is the longest, emptying into the Black Sea. Van Gölü (Lake Van) is the largest in Turkey, but its waters are saline, as are those of another large body of water, Lake Tuz.

Climate in both Greece and Turkey is predominantly Mediterranean, with long, hot summers, and mild, wet winters. Athens and Istanbul have an average temperature ranging from 10°C (37–48°F) in January, to 28°C (83°F) in July, with heaviest rains between October and March. Snow is common in the mountains of northern Greece and the western side of the Pindus Mountains receives most of the rainfall. Vegetation, abundant in Greece of ancient times, has been significantly depleted, but remains diverse depending on the elevation. Nowadays, up to 30 percent of Greek territory consists of cultivated fields and orchards, with oranges, olives, dates, pomegranates, figs, cotton and tobacco, deciduous and evergreen forests growing up to altitudes of 1,200m (4,000ft); wild flowers are found up to 1,500m (5,000ft) and mosses and lichens predominate at higher elevations. The area is generally lacking other natural resources and is limited to small deposits of bauxite, asbestos, nickel, magnesite, marble, black coal. Air and water pollution in the Athens area are major issues, heavily damaging not only nature but also classic Greek antiquities in and outside the city.

While much of the Aegean and Mediterranean shores of Turkey enjoy the same climate as Greece, the central Anatolian Plateau has a continental climate with hot summers and cold winters and the eastern highlands experience even longer and colder winters, where pastoralism and grazing have prevailed for thousands of years. Moreover, there are very few forests around most of the Anatolian Peninsula, except for alpine vegetation at higher elevations.

Finally, only wild boar remains abundant in this area: wolf, fox, wildcat, hyena, jackal, deer, bear, marten and mountain goat meanwhile only inhabit the more remote areas, while camel, water buffalo and Angora goat have been domesticated. Bird life is rich, with wild goose, partridge and quail dominating the skies, while migration birds pass through Bosporus. Contrary to Greece, Turkey had a number of small but important mineral deposits, such as coal and iron ore, chromium, high-grade magnetite, lead and zinc. Significant reserves of gas have been discovered in the north-eastern

Mediterranean in the last decade, but their ownership is disputed and are a source of current diplomatic and military disputes.

Early History
Southern Europe and the Anatolian Peninsula – comprising modern-day Greece and Turkey – are some of the oldest, permanently settled regions of the world; the history of human population in these areas can be traced back to around 210,000 years ago, when humans began spreading from Africa. Eastern Thrace has been inhabited since at least 40,000 years ago, while a pre-pottery Neolithic temple with world's oldest known megaliths – massive carved stones – unearthed at Göbekli Tepe, outside Urfa in south-eastern Turkey, has been dated to between 9500 to 8000 BCE thus predating Stonehenge by around 6,000 years.

Both the territories of Greece and Turkey have been home to ethnically and culturally distinct groups from the ancient Hittites, Phrygians and Assyrians, to Greeks, Persians, Romans, and Arabs. The area nowadays within the borders of the Hellenic Republic, was under the control of the Cycladic civilisation (around 3200 BCE), the Minoan civilisation (2700–1500 BCE), and then the Mycenaean civilisation (1600–1100 BCE).

Following several centuries of the so-called Dark Ages, a myriad of kingdoms and city-states emerged across the southern Balkans and the Greek peninsula, eventually spreading along the shores from south-eastern Spain, southern France, southern Italy, to Minor Asia and the Black Sea. As they reached high levels of prosperity, the result was an unprecedented cultural boom, expressed in architecture, drama, science, mathematics and philosophy, followed in 508 BCE, by the emergence of the world's first democratic system of government in Athens.

In the year 500 BCE, the area found itself exposed to an invasion of the Persian Empire, in reaction to which the Hellenic League was established, in 481 BCE – the first historically recorded union of Greek states. Its victory in the Hellenic-Persian Wars was followed by more than 50 years of peace, known as the Golden Age of Athens. It came to an end due to the political disunity, which resulted in the devastating Peloponnesian War of 431–404 BCE, the end of which marked the beginning of the rise of Macedonia as the leading power of the League of Corinth. The most famous ruler of the subsequent period was Alexander III ('The Great'), who in 334 BCE, launched an expansion in eastern and southern direction. By the time of his death, in 323 BCE, he created one of largest empires in history, stretching from the Ionian Sea to the eastern side of the Indus River.

Subsequently, between 276 and 146 BCE, Greek city-states gradually came under the control of the Roman Republic, completed in 27 BCE through their full annexation. The Romans greatly admired and became heavily influenced by the Greek culture, widely adapting its principles. In turn, through the 2nd and 3rd centuries, the Greek-speaking communities of the Hellenised east were instrumental in the spread of early Christianity, although pagan religions were widely followed until outlawed in 391–392. Following the fall of the Western Roman Empire, in the fifth century, Greece remained under the control of the former Eastern Roman Empire, now the Byzantine Empire, with its capital in Constantinople. Known as the 'Kingdom of Romans' in its time, this largely retained the Greek language and culture, while developing the Eastern Orthodox Christian religion.

Meanwhile, Proto-Turks emerged in Central Eastern Asia, probably in the Altai-Sayan region, Mongolia or Tuva, and their existence was first recorded in written format in China of the sixth century. While nomadic people, they traded wool, leather, carpets, horses and iron for grain, silk, wood, vegetables, and gradually entered the Altai Mountains area, where many were targeted by Arabic raids and began converting to Islam under influence of the Persians. By the ninth century, Turkish officers began serving with armies of the Abbasid Caliphate. Strongly influenced by Persian civilisation, the Seljuk Turks spread and took over the eastern provinces of the Abbasid Empire in the eleventh century, captured Baghdad and made their first incursions into Anatolia. After defeating the Byzantine Empire in the Battle of Manzikert, in 1071, they spread into the Anatolian Peninsula, gradually transforming it from predominantly Christian and Greek-speaking to a mostly Muslim and Turkish-speaking one.

Ottoman Conquests

The Ottoman Empire was founded in the late thirteenth century in north-western Anatolia by the tribal leader Osman I. By 1354, it crossed into Europe and initiated a conquest of the Balkans. Macedonia, Serbia and Bulgaria were overrun by the 1430s and the Crusade of Varna defeated in 1444. This advance made the issue of Constantinople important: the Byzantine Empire was already weakened by the sack of its capital by the Latins in 1204 and the Black Death and was exhausted both demographically and militarily. After reorganising his rapidly expanding state, Mehmed the Conqueror captured the city in 1453. Most of Greece followed by 1460, leaving only Cyprus and Crete under Venetian control.

While considering the Greek Orthodox Church and the Ecumenical Patriarchate of Constantinople (officially renamed Istanbul in the 1920s) as the ruling authorities of the entire conquered Christian population of the area (irrespective of these being ethnically Greek or not) and allowing it to maintain its autonomy and land in exchange for accepting his authority, the Ottomans did not force non-Muslims to convert to Islam. Indeed – although the nature of their administration varied greatly from municipality to municipality (with some places being arbitrary and harsh, and elsewhere effectively autonomous from the central rule) – the majority of the Orthodox population greatly preferred the Ottoman rule to that of Venice. Foremost, Greeks living on the islands of the Ionian Sea lived in prosperity, while those in Istanbul achieved positions of power within the Ottoman administration.

The expansion of the Ottoman Empire was continued by the highly committed and effective sultans of the sixteenth century, peaking in the defeat of the Mamluks that secured it Syria and Egypt in 1520–1521, and – after the victory in the Battle of Mohac, in 1521 – Hungary. Moreover, they pushed conquests all the way to Algeria, took Baghdad from the Persians in 1535, reached the Persian Gulf and expanded down the Red Sea. Through additional conquests in the Adriatic, Aegean and Morea and through an alliance with France, the empire grew into a dominant naval force in the Mediterranean Sea. The growth in power and influence of the Iberian Union and its discovery of new maritime trade routes to India and the Far East, initiated a series of Ottoman-Portuguese naval wars in the Indian Ocean, eventually prompting Istanbul to deploy an expeditionary force to its easternmost territory, the Sultanate of Aceh.

However, this conflict ended in a stalemate and the Ottomans meanwhile experienced several defeats, including the first siege of Vienna (1529), on Malta (1565), on Venetian Cyprus (1537 and 1570–1571), and at Lepanto (1571). That said, over the following 300 years, Ottomans exercised control over a huge empire stretching from modern-day Ukraine in the north, to Yemen in the south, and from Algeria in the west to the lower Persian Gulf in the east. This prospered and flourished economically due to trade between the East and the West, and a system of administration that followed peaceful coexistence; every ethno-religious minority constituted a *millet*, its own community.

Residing in Istanbul, Ottoman sultans claimed the title of Caliph for themselves, which made them the religious leaders of all the Sunni Muslims. However, thanks to the *millet* system, not only did large communities of Christians, Jews and other religious groups survive, but were actually granted considerable autonomy (for comparison: the Shi'a Muslims were considered 'heretics'). The Ottomans intervened only whenever they were suspicious of loyalty or when facing popular complaints against local rulers.

Despite the growing European presence in the Indian Ocean, Ottoman trade with the east continued to flourish and new conquests were launched into eastern Europe and Russia. In 1683, Grand Vezir Kara Mustafa Pasha made the mistake of launching a campaign that culminated in the second siege of Vienna, in Austria. His forces were swept away by allied Habsburg, German and Polish forces spearheaded by the Polish King John II Sobieski, and then defeated in the Great Turkish War, which ended only with the Treaty of Karlowitz, in 1699.

Contrary to stories created by the British and French propaganda of the nineteenth century about the Ottoman Empire entering a period of decline, the state continued to maintain a strong economy thanks to continuously flourishing trade with Asia. Indeed, even the Ottoman rule over the Balkans remained stable and the empire remained successful in defeating the Austrian and Russian expansions of the eighteenth century. It was only the decades of peace – from 1740 until 1768 – that resulted in the Ottoman armed forces falling behind those of their European Rivals.

The Longest Century

During the centuries of expansion, the Ottoman armed forces went through five major reforms, developing from their 'classic' form of a steppe-nomadic cavalry force, into a mix of the Janissary infantry, Sipahi cavalry and auxiliary forces, supported by mobile artillery. A disastrous defeat in the war with the Russian Empire, in 1768–1774, demonstrated that this was not enough. In 1798, France invaded the Ottoman Province of Egypt and in a single battle, destroyed an Ottoman Army led by the Mamluks. Although Napoleon Bonaparte then failed to establish himself in lasting control over Egypt, the campaign to recover the province proved a troublesome process.

Simultaneously, trouble was brewing in the Sanjak of Smederevo, in the Balkans, where the population was suffering from Janissary terror. Whilst sympathetic to his Serbian subjects, the Nizam reforms pre-dated Mehmed Ali, who was if anything influenced by Selim's early effort at creating it (see Shaw). Along with what he had seen of British and French troops in Egypt. Later Ottoman military reforms did recognise that Ali had achieved what they had not, until the Janissaries were dissolved.

However, while setting a pattern of importing Western military technology and knowledge that was to recur throughout the nineteenth century, this effort backfired: in cooperation with the Ottoman religious leadership, the Janissary Corps defeated the Serbian uprising, but also toppled the Sultan and disbanded the New Order Army in 1807. For the next 19 years, the new Sultan Mahmud II was preoccupied with securing his own position, while the Serbs launched their second and then third uprising, eventually forcing Istanbul to enter negotiations. In 1830, the Principality of Serbia was recognised as an autonomous part of the Ottoman Empire.

Meanwhile, Mehmed Ali's success against the French only caused yet more trouble: it swept the eastern Mediterranean free of French merchants, thus enabling a rapid expansion of a wealthy merchant class in Greece. In turn, the Greeks established contacts with the Empire of Russia, which was on a search for investment and know-how for its recently conquered new possessions in the Black Sea.

In 1821, almost simultaneously with a revolt of the Islamic fundamentalist Wahhabis of Arabia, led by the Saud family, an Odesa-based exile organisation of Greeks set up an armed uprising against the Ottoman rule, provoking the Greek War of Independence. Shipped to Greece, Mehmed Ali's army (led by his son Ibrahim Pasha) defeated the insurgency that was divided due to political differences. However, reports about its massacres of the civilian population galvanised public opinion in Europe in the Greek favour and prompted Great Britain, France and the Russian Empire into an intervention. In 1827, the First Hellenic Republic was proclaimed and the nascent state was officially recognised under the London Protocol of 1830.

Arguably, the Greece of the time was independent on paper only; it controlled the Attica region and the Peloponnese peninsula and was completely dependent on Western protection for its survival. Moreover, its population was deeply divided about its political organisation and was destabilised by continuous unrest and assassinations. When the West attempted to stabilise the situation through installing Bavarian Prince Otto von Wittelsbach as monarch in Athens, his despotic rule further increased the tension. It was only after a military coup of 1909 that Greece underwent sweeping constitutional, fiscal, social, and military reforms that brought some stability.

In 1826, Sultan Mahmud II won a major power struggle in Istanbul and destroyed the 135,000-strong Janissary Corps in bloodshed. However, his subsequent reforms were slowed down by the cost of recruiting, training and equipping a modern army. Moreover, the successful struggle of Serbs and Greeks and the Russian Empire declaring itself the protector of Orthodox Christianity in the Rumeli (Ottoman-administered Balkan), then emboldened independence movements in Romania and Bulgaria, while the Ottoman Empire found itself facing multiple new threats.

The rapidly industrialised Great Britain had a fundamental interest in securing the Mediterranean as the shortest route to its colonial possessions in India. The Russians defeated the Ottomans in another war of 1827–1828, while the former ally France, exploited the opportunity to conquer Algeria and Tunisia in 1830–1831. Finally, emboldened by rapid economic growth of Egypt under his rule, Mehmed Ali launched a mutiny against Istanbul that escalated into the First Egyptian-Ottoman War of 1831–1833, followed by the Second, in 1838–1840, in turn sparking an era of national awakening and the gradual loss of control over large parts of the empire in the Balkans and parts of the Middle East.

In 1839, Mahmud II died and his son Abdulmejid I became the Sultan. Promoted by the reformist Grand Vizier Mustafa Resid Pasha, Abdulmejid initiated another period of comprehensive reforms and modernisation, best-known as the *Tanzimat*. Lasting until 1876, this resulted in constitutional reforms, establishment of a modern conscript army and the replacement of religious law by secular law, build-up of the schooling system, emergence of a modern banking system and industrialisation. For a while, Abdulmajid was successful in selection of his allies abroad and during the next showdown with Russia, in form of the Crimean War of 1853–1856, the Ottoman Empire found itself on the side of victors. However, this had no lasting consequences – foremost because Istanbul was heavily indebted to Western creditors at a time when the economy was heavily strained due to the flight of millions of Muslims from eastern Europe.

Abdulmejid I died in 1861 and was followed by two less-successful sultans, both dominated by grand viziers and other high bureaucrats. It was only in 1876 that Abdul Hamid II ascended the throne and gave a new impetus to modernisation – first through promulgating the constitution and a parliament. However, such ideas of this 'dangerous reformer' were strongly opposed not only from within, but especially by Great Britain, France and Russia who assumed that their civilisation was superior to what they perceived as (and partially were) 'negative attributes' and outright 'barbarity' of the Ottoman Muslims. Although the British initially propped up the Ottomans as a 'bulwark against Russia', all three empires repeatedly conspired to not only destroy the empire but even its legacy, and thus fostered political turmoil and embroil it in another series of wars.

In 1875–1876, a new wave of uprisings against Ottoman rule erupted in Herzegovina, then Bosnia and finally in Bulgaria, even though the Ottomans defeated Serbia in 1876. Meanwhile, shaken by defeat in the Crimean War, but determined to recover its territorial losses, the Russian Empire concluded an alliance with the Austro-Hungarian Empire, Bulgaria, Romania, Serbia and Montenegro. The resulting coalition won the Russo-Turkish War of 1877–1878; the principalities of Romania, Serbia and Montenegro all proclaimed independence, the Principality of Bulgaria emerged as an autonomous state, while Russia re-established itself as the dominant power in the Black Sea. Indeed, the fighting stopped only

Sultan Abdul Hamid II as seen in 1867. (Albert Grandolini Collection)

through an intervention of Western powers, concerned about the Russians possibly reaching the Mediterranean.

The conflict had tremendous consequences for the Ottoman Empire. Not only had London convinced a bankrupt Istanbul to lease the island of Cyprus for an annual rent and a guarantee that Great Britain would protect the Ottoman capital against a possible Russian invasion; more importantly, between five and seven million Muslims had either left or were expelled from the areas that had broken away or were taken away from the Ottoman Empire. Understanding he could not ignore the need to protect Muslims and concluding that the situation threatened the very survival of his state, in 1877 Abdul Hamid II dissolved the parliament and usurped all the political powers.

The dust over the Russo-Turkish War of 1877–1878 had not even settled when Great Britain made its next move: in 1882, under the pretext of 'helping the Ottoman government' in putting down a revolt of Egyptian and Sudanese forces in which up to 50 Europeans were killed, securing its interests and investments and safeguarding the Suez Canal, Great Britain invaded and conquered Egypt. At first, warships of the Royal Navy destroyed much of Alexandria by shelling the city with high-explosive shells from 11 to 13 July, killing hundreds – if not thousands – of civilians. In August, a force of 40,000 then landed in the Suez Canal Zone before advancing on Cairo and defeating defenders in the course of the Battles of Kfar el-Dawwar and Tell el-Kebir.

Entirely ignored in Europe at the time (and ever since) was the fact that regardless of internal conflicts between Cairo and Istanbul and despite local independence demands, Egypt was still a part of the Ottoman Empire and one playing a crucial role in the modernisation of the country. Unsurprisingly, while hailed as a great achievement in peace-making and stabilisation, this invasion created grievances that were to explode into the face of Western powers several decades later.

Sultan Abdul Hamid II took care to recreate an absolutist regime. His principal problem was the issue of bringing the disparate population of the empire towards a common identity through adoption of a new ideological principle – the Ottoman Pan Islamism – as a means of countering European influence. This idea was supported by the fact that the proportion of Christians in the empire had significantly declined due to the Russian and Egyptian invasions, while the proportion of Muslims had increased due to the arrival of millions of refugees, making Islam – for the first time – overwhelmingly preponderant in the Ottoman Empire. In turn, refugees had bitter experiences about the fate of Muslims in emerging Christian nation-states under Russian and British occupation and thus, became disproportionally represented among the supporters of the new ideology.

Abdul Hamid also introduced reforms in the economy and education. A large network of carefully maintained roads and modern railways – the latter spanned more than 10,000km by 1914 – was constructed, followed by the largest telegraph network in the world, connecting every town and employing an army of technicians and specialists capable of transmitting messages in at least a dozen languages. Through the early twentieth century, all the cities and towns were provided with electricity. Parallel to this process a huge, state-controlled education system emerged, based on the construction of elementary, secondary and primary schools all over the Ottoman Empire (indeed, every village received an elementary school).

The economic reforms and improved education resulted not only in a flourishing economy, but also in flourishing journalism. Although the press was censored, the journalists introduced ever more advanced ideas from the West, influencing the emergence of multiple political and nationalist movements – including a group of young dissidents organised as the Committee of Union & Progress (CUP; colloquially 'Young Turks', although the movement involved many Arabs, Albanians, Jews and – initially – Armenians and Greeks).

In 1908, the CUP forced Abdul Hamid II to restore a constitutional monarchy with a parliament, abolish censorship and release all political prisoners. The new constitution re-established an inclusive

Constructed in 1829, and equipped with 128 guns on three decks, the ship of the line *Mahmudiye* was the largest warship in the world for decades. She saw action in numerous conflicts, including the Greek War of Independence, the Crimean War of 1854–1855 and the Russo-Turkish War of 1877–1878, but was rapidly rendered obsolete by technological advances. (Piri Reis History Research Centre)

governing system in which inhabitants from all ethnic and religious groups elected their municipal and provincial councils and the old and rich tradition of Ottoman citizens addressing their grievances to the state in the form of petitions – in which they could protest everything from official corruption and police brutality to bad service from local officials. Not only Sultan Abdul Hamid II, but also the Young Turks and every provincial governor, were conscious to always react to every complaint carefully. Once again, the instability in the Ottoman Empire was exploited by foreign powers: the Austro-Hungarian Empire seized the opportunity to annex the province of Bosnia and Herzegovina, which it had occupied since 1878, while Bulgaria formally declared independence and was internationally recognised.

The reforms introduced by Abdul Hamid and the Young Turks still left the empire lagging behind the Western powers regarding industrialisation, even behind the Russian Empire. Foremost, the Ottoman Empire had accumulated a huge foreign debt and was completely dependent on ever more foreign loans for survival. Nevertheless and while the authorities worked hard on establishing a common Ottoman identity, diverse ethnic and religious groups not only enjoyed their own rights and privileges but created opportunities for their economic prosperity – always based on meritocracy.

14 Years of War

If Abdul Hamid II was successful in anything, it was keeping his empire out of any major international disputes. Numerous uprisings did erupt in the Balkans and on the island of Crete in the 1880s and 1890s, but the Ottoman Empire was not embroiled in a new war. In 1911, Italy exploited Istanbul's preoccupation with a revolt in Yemen and invaded and captured the Vilayet of Tripoli (modern-day northern Libya), and the Dodecanese islands in the Aegean Sea. Rome officially 'agreed to return' the Dodecanese through the Treaty of Ouchy in 1912, but the vagueness of the text, combined with subsequent events, made sure that the 'provisional' Italian administration remained in power.

Foremost, sensing Ottoman weakness and motivated by growing nationalism, in 1912–1913, Greece, Serbia, Montenegro and Bulgaria declared war upon the Ottoman Empire and defeated it, conquering nearly all of its European provinces bar the Eastern Thrace. This conflict – the First Balkan War – was not only marked by massive actions of ethnic cleansing and grave atrocities against civilians that drove additional millions of refugees into the empire, but was quickly followed by the Second Balkan War of 1913, in which Greece, Serbia and Romania, followed by the Ottomans, defeated Bulgaria. The situation was soon to worsen due to the outbreak of the First World War, in late July and early August 1914; a conflict that put both Greece and the Ottoman Empire into a precarious situation.

Nominally, both nations were neutral, just like their arch-rival Bulgaria. However, as the Great War went on, warring camps emerged both in Athens and in Istanbul, the influence of which created deep rifts in local societies. Following decades of political instability, Greece emerged victorious out of the two Balkan Wars, nearly doubling its territory and population through the annexation of Crete, Epirus, and Macedonia. However, this success led to another rift in Athens: this time between royalist pro-Germans and the pro-Entente politicians in Thessaloniki. Led by Prime Minister Elftherios Venizelos, the latter were supportive of an entry in the war, but King Constantine I – who had been educated in Germany, married to Kaiser Wilhelm II's sister, and was a big admirer of Prussian militarism – anticipated a German victory: merely his awareness that Greece was vulnerable to the possible invasions of France and Great Britain prompted him to advocate a course of neutrality.

In Istanbul, much of the CUP-government was leaning towards Germany too, if for no other reason than because of the British

Ottoman Army gunners with a German-made leichte Fehldhaubitze 98 in position. (Albert Grandolini Collection)

occupations of Cyprus and Egypt. However, such viewpoints were strongly opposed by some of the Young Turks who staged several attacks on the German Military Mission and organised numerous anti-war protests. That said, the country remained stable and under the control of the Minister of War, Ismail Enver (better known as Enver Pasha) whose government eventually decided to side with the Central Powers. On 29 October 1914, the Ottoman Empire entered the war by carrying out a surprise attack on the Black Sea coast of Russia, prompting Moscow to declare war on 2 November, after which Istanbul declared war on the Entente. London reacted with formal annexation of Cyprus but, only a few months later, offered the island to Athens – on condition that Greece joined the Entente. Although repeated several times, this offer was declined and eventually withdrawn.

On the frontlines, and rather unexpectedly for the Western powers, the Ottoman armed forces fared quite well. In the north, they lost some ground (and lots of troops) in the Caucasus, before the armistice of Erzincan ended the fighting on 5 December 1917. Nevertheless, the fighting between the Ottomans and Armenians went on well into 1920. In the south, the Ottomans launched an advance over the Sinai Peninsula in direction of the Suez Canal, but this was stopped by the British in February 1915. Meanwhile, the British captured Basra in southern Mesopotamia and then marched on Baghdad – only to be stopped at Ctesphon, in November 1915, and then heavily defeated at al-Qut, in April 1916. The situation in Mesopotamia was still heating up when, on 19 February 1915, a combined Franco-British fleet attempted to force a passage through the Dardanelles with the aim of conquering Istanbul. This effort failed but was followed by an amphibious landing on the Gallipoli peninsula, with the aim of taking control of the Ottoman Straits and resuming the advance on Istanbul. After eight months of bitter fighting, this campaign ended nowhere, the troops involved suffered heavy losses and hardships and the invasion force was evacuated. The two Ottoman victories not only embittered the British, but propelled the career of General Mustafa Kemal, who was widely hailed as the saviour of the empire.

Elsewhere, the Ottoman Army in Palestine successfully defended during the First and Second Battles of Gaza, in early 1917, but then lost Beersheba, followed by Jerusalem, in November and December of the same year. Already weakened by the British-supported Arab uprising, in 1918, it then lost three armies during the battles of Sharon, Nablus and in Transjordan. By October, it withdrew from Damascus and Aleppo and was on retreat towards the north when the fighting – temporarily – ended with the Armistice of Mudros, on 30 October 1918.

Nothing similar happened in Greece. On the contrary, the dispute between Venizelos and the king reached a point where the country was split into two. Venizelos and his supporters won the elections of 1915 and – in reaction to London's offer of 'territorial expansion into Asia Minor' – called the British and French to deploy their troops in the Thessaloniki area. The reaction was prompt: while an Anglo-French contingent established a defence perimeter around the port, the French occupied the island of Corfu, where the survivors of the defeated Serbian Army were gathered for rest and reorganisation.

King Constantine – supported by much of the population – was outraged; he reacted with an unconstitutional dismissal of the government and the parliament before, in May 1916, making a major mistake and ordering a surrender of Fort Rupel, in northern

Eleftherios Venizelos, one of the most significant politicians of modern Greece. (Albert Grandolini Collection)

Macedonia, to a combined German-Bulgarian force which thus, captured the entire IV Army Corps. It was only the Bulgarian invasion of eastern Macedonia, in August of the same year, that opened the way out; it prompted a coup from within the armed forces, parts of which sided with the provisional government led by Venizelos in Thessaloniki.

For a while, the net result was two Greek states: the Entente-supported provisional government in Thessaloniki, which controlled most of Macedonia, Crete and the northern Aegean islands, and the royalist government controlling the rest of the country, the so-called 'Old Greece'. A solution was found only in May 1917, when Great Britain and France decided to invoke their 'obligation as protecting powers' of the Hellenic Kingdom from 1832 and demanded the king's resignation. Constantine accepted and went into exile in Switzerland, leaving his son Alexander on the throne. Back in Athens, Venizelos then deployed the armed forces on the side of the Entente. The presence of 300,000 fresh Greek troops eventually altered the balance between the opponents on the Macedonian front. Under the command of French General Franche d'Espèrey in September 1918, the combined British, French, Greek and Serbian forces defeated Bulgaria in the September Offensive and the Battle of Dobro Pole, forcing Sofia out of the war. Subsequently, the Allies pushed into Serbia and liberated all of it by October 1918. At the time of the armistice that brought the First World War to an end, they were in the process of preparing an invasion of Hungary.

Great Disaster

During the final days of the First World War, between 30 October and 1 November 1922, British, French and Italian troops invaded the Ottoman Empire and occupied Istanbul. The Ottoman government collapsed almost entirely, its officials fleeing in an eastern direction, while what was left in the capital was persuaded to suspend the constitution and dissolve the parliament. However, Great Britain and France were still not satisfied; aiming to partition the empire and establish their domination over most of the Anatolian Peninsula and the entire Middle East, they implemented earlier agreements (foremost the Sykes-Picot Treaty of 1916) and continued their advance for weeks longer. Moreover, in May 1919, they persuaded Prime Minister Venizelos to deploy a 'peacekeeping force' of 20,000 Greek Army troops and occupy Ayvalik and Izmir on the eastern coast of the Aegean Sea, under the pretext of 'maintaining stability in the region.' Furthermore, during the Paris Peace Conference, the Armenian Diaspora managed to convince US President Wilson to grant a large part of north-eastern Ottoman Empire to the Democratic Republic of Armenia.

As a result, in 1920 the Western powers forced the Ottoman government to sign the Treaty of Sèvres, massively unfavourable to its own interests; western Anatolia was to be given to Greece, south-western to Italy, an Armenian state was to emerge in eastern Anatolia, while the

French troops in Athens, with Acropolis in the background, in 1917. (*Grosser Bilderatlas des Weltkrieges*)

Ottoman cavalry on the march south of Jerusalem, in 1917. (Albert Grandolini Collection)

territories further south – the Ottoman *Vilayet of Suriyya* (modern-day Syria, Palestine/Israel, Jordan and north-western Saudi Arabia) – were to be reorganised into British- and French-controlled 'mandates'.

However, the presence of Western powers and the flight of millions of refugees, followed by the arrival of the Greek Army, inflamed ethnic tensions, caused widespread civil disobedience and eventually, an insurgency that opposed the occupants. In another ill-advised act, the short-lived government, led by Sultan Mehmed VI, reacted by dispatching highly-respected Mustafa Kemal to Anatolia to restore order. Once there, the general discovered that large areas in the north, east and south, were in a state of practical anarchy, depopulated or troubled by massive migration and widespread banditry. Nevertheless, large units of the Ottoman Army remained intact as British and French prosecution of CUP-members caused massive dissent between its officers and they refused to disarm and demobilise, while others reorganised into a range of diverse militias. The result was the next armed conflict, known under different designations between other participants – for example, as the Asia

Minor Campaign in Greece – but foremost as the Turkish War of Independence in Turkey.

This war was fought on several widely separated frontlines from 1919 until 1922. In the east, the reorganised XV Corps of the Ottoman Army and Kurdish militia, supported by shipments of gold and arms from the nascent Union of the Soviet Socialist Republics (USSR; colloquially 'Soviet Union'), the defeated Armenians and launched an advance on Yerevan, the fall of which was pre-empted only by the Soviet Red Army's invasion of Armenia from the east. The fighting was concluded by the Treaty of Alexandropol, of December 1920, in which Armenians were forced to renounce the Treaty of Sèvres. In the west, during the summer of 1920, and after numerous attacks on their positions, Greece – encouraged by Great Britain – launched an offensive aiming to force the Turkish nationalists in Ankara to sign the Treaty of Sèvres.

Financed by Great Britain and France, the Greek Army defeated Turkish irregulars in the Battle of Kütahya-Eskisehir and then launched an advance on the nationalist stronghold in Ankara, in central Anatolia. However, it overstretched its supply lines in the process, enabling reorganised Ottoman forces, under Mustafa Kemal, to check its advance in the Battle of Sakarya and then counterattack in the Great Offensive; the latter drove the Greeks out of Anatolia in a matter of just three weeks.

After the Turks recovered Izmir (and torched most of the city, killing thousands in the process), Athens was forced into signing the armistice of Mudanya, in October 1922. Meanwhile, the French Army deployed to secure all of Syria and Cilicia, was defeated and forced to withdraw to Aleppo by a Turkish nationalist uprising of 1920–1921. Firmly in control, Mustafa Kemal then expelled the last Ottoman Sultan from Istanbul and officially rejected the Treaty of Sèvres. Indeed, realising they could not bring the situation under control without another major war, the British, French, Greek, Italian, Romanian and Serbian governments were left without a choice but to negotiate a new agreement with his government: the Treaty of Lausanne of 24 July 1923. Instead of division of Ottoman territories and while providing for unrestricted civilian and non-military passage through the Turkish Straits, this officially recognised the Mustafa Kemal-led Turkish National Movement and its sovereignty, over all of Anatolian Peninsula, Istanbul, Cilicia and Eastern Thrace.

Another result being that the Greek and Turkish governments agreed to engage in 'a population exchange' which ran amid widespread atrocities against civilians of both sides. The resulting exodus turned into a catastrophe of incredible proportions (considered a 'genocide' in Armenia and Greece), the effects of which created immense hatred and are strongly felt until this very day.

Slow Recovery

After more than 15 years of power struggles, military coups and especially wars, both Greece and the dying Ottoman Empire were in ruins, their populations decimated but swollen by millions of traumatised refugees, many of whom did not even speak the native language, and had no affiliations with their new homelands. Neither was to experience any respite.

Following victorious conclusion of the Turkish War of Independence, Mustafa Kemal first took care to secure the borders of his new, sovereign country named Turkey. This he managed in the form of the Treaty of Lausanne. Three months later, on 29 October of the same year, the Grand National Assembly in Ankara voted for a new constitution that declared a republic, with Mustapha Kemal – who took the family name Atatürk ('Father of Turks') when the National Assembly introduced the surname law, in 1934 – as the first president. Finally, on 3 March 1924 – and much to disappointment of not only many of Atatürk's followers, but especially many Arabs in the Middle East, now left under the brutal British and French colonial rule – the Grand National Assembly abolished the Caliphate, and the next day Sultan Abdulmajid II left Istanbul, thus ending 640 years of the Ottoman Empire.

Subsequently, Atatürk and the Grand National Assembly launched major efforts to modernise the country through political, economic and social reforms. Originally, Kemal was aiming to establish a secular parliamentary democracy, however, this altered over the following years as the nascent nation required an immense amount of reconstruction and was facing powerful challenges from the supporters of the Ottoman regime and clergy and also new ideologies like communism and fascism. Eventually, Atatürk permitted the activity of only one party; his Grand National Assembly, renamed the Republican People's Party, established during the Turkish War of Independence. Nevertheless, parliamentary elections were otherwise free and used an egalitarian

Greek Army troops entering Izmir (Smyrne), in May 1919. (Albert Grandolini Collection)

system based on a general ballot. The Turkish Constitution of 1924 dismantled the Ottoman bureaucracy, separated the powers between the legislative and the executive branches of the state and these two from the judiciary system. The result was a new ideology of Kemalism: a mix of Republicanism, Nationalism, Popularism, and Revolutionism, delivered through Secularism and Statism and aiming to unite the Turkish people around one common goal: the creation of a modern state.

The resulting political order was no western democracy, but also no fascistic dictatorship as subsequently emerged in Italy and Germany. Nowhere was this as obvious as on the international scene, where Atatürk's government pursued the policy of maintaining neutrality and a status quo. On the domestic front, the new republic introduced extensive social, cultural, and economic reforms, the most radical of which was removing religion from the political realm. The emancipation of women, a new alphabet, land reform, economic plans and even a new interpretation of the history of the Turks, were driven forward and all these changes were introduced at a remarkable pace, despite some resistance within political and military circles. Within the international plan, Atatürk lost the diplomatic struggle for the *Vilayet of Mosul*, to the British, who despite predominant wishes of the local population, secured the latter for Iraq. In turn, the strongman in Ankara gained Hatay from the French (in July 1938) and established friendly relations with Moscow and the USSR.

The situation in Greece of the 1920s was dramatically different. Greek Prime Minister Venizelos earned the reputation of being an international statesman of considerable stature due to his victory over the Royalists, the triumph through the Treaty of Neuilly with Bulgaria, the successful conclusion of the First World War, the British promise of territorial gains at the expense of the Ottoman Empire and his participation in the Paris Peace Conference of 1919. However, at home these victories brought him nothing but trouble. On the contrary, the abuse of power by him and his aides and their fierce prosecution of their political opposition, led to the extremism of the latter. Moreover, in October 1919, King Alexander died, reviving the ongoing dispute of whether the country should be a monarchy or a republic.

The war-weariness of the population – much of which was mobilised since 1912 – prevailed and during the elections in November 1919, anti-Venzielists won the majority. However, the Great Disaster of 1919–1921 led to a temporary abolition of the monarchy – via referendum – in 1924 and a declaration of the Second Hellenic Republic. This was short-lived; in 1936, the monarchist General Ioannis Metaxas established himself as prime minister of a dictatorial regime, with King George II as the head of state – now officially the Kingdom of Greece.

That said, and despite fierce animosities, both the Greek and Turkish governments went to quite some extremes to normalise their relations, Eventually, both renounced all claims over each other's territory and in 1930, concluded a corresponding agreement. Three years later, relations between Athens and Ankara reached a level where the two governments signed a comprehensive treaty called the Entente Cordiale, which became the stepping stone for the Balkan Pact, joined by Romania and Yugoslavia, in 1934, as a united front against Bulgarian designs on territories of its members.

The Second World War and After

The Second World War, which began with the Nazi German invasion of Poland, on 1 September 1939, came in between a further improvement of relations. About a year later, while preparing its invasion of the USSR, Berlin forced the government in Bucharest into the Treaty of Craiova. This effectively excluded Romania from the Balkan Pact; when Yugoslavia then signed the Tripartite Pact with the Axis powers in March 1941, the defence alliance in the Balkans was null and void. From that point onwards, histories of Greece and Turkey went their own way.

While Turkey avoided being dragged into the Second World War until 1945, in October 1940, Greece found itself at the receiving end of an Italian invasion. With British military support, the Greek armed forces defeated the Italians, but in April 1941, then quickly succumbed to the German invasion. The occupation brought terrible hardship for the civilian population; thousands starved during the winter of 1941–1942, and dozens of thousands fell victim to reprisals for disobedience by Nazis and collaborators. The situation further worsened due to the Greek Resistance, which fought amongst themselves. The German, Bulgarian and Italian occupiers committed numerous atrocities, including mass executions and wholesale destruction of towns and villages, leaving almost one million homeless. Nevertheless, the exiled elements of the Greek armed forces were reformed and fought with the Allies in North Africa and the Middle East (including at El Alamein), in Italy and in the Aegean Sea.

The two countries thus emerged from the turbulent 1940s in an entirely different condition. A multi-party system was established in Turkey mid-way through the decade, based around two parties. However, the country was still short of becoming a fully-functioning democracy of the Western type and the stability of its government was always guaranteed by the military's role in political life. The Republican People's Party (RPP) represented the intelligentsia, favouring state-directed reform, while the Democratic Party (DP; renamed the Justice Party after 1960) drew support from small towns and peasants. A new constitution of 1961 resulted in the growth of additional, smaller parties driven by ideology from the extreme left, to Islamic fundamentalists, who could hold the balance of power between the two main parties and influence policy. However, later during that decade, the Turkish political landscape become more polarised and violent. Turkish nationalism was secular and unlike many Arab countries, largely devoid of anti-western feelings; that said, religion continued to play an important role in the life of individual citizens.

In Greece, the establishment of the Metaxas regime in 1936 inaugurated a period of authoritarian rule that was to last until 1974. Following the Axis withdrawal of 1944, Greece regained western Thrace from Bulgaria but was denied the northern Epirus despite the Allied promise in this regard. Instead, the Dodecanese Islands – which were brought under British control and then declared a military protectorate – were awarded to Greece in the Treaty of Paris of 1947. However, the country then descended into a bloody civil war between communist forces supported by Yugoslavia, Bulgaria, and Albania, and the British, and then US-supported, reactionary regime. Although this concluded with the victory of the latter, this conflict caused further economic devastation, mass population displacement and severe polarisation of the society, which continued through the 1950s. Greece survived foremost thanks to the economic aid provided by the USA within the frame of the Marshal Plan – and into the 1960s, culminating in a coup d'état of 21 April 1967 by the 'Regime of the Colonels'. In 1968, the resulting military junta established a new constitution, defining the country as a 'crowned democracy'. However, it suspended elections to parliament and appointed both a prime minister and a (largely military) cabinet: all civil rights were suspended, and repression and abuse became rampant.

2
HELLENIC ARMED FORCES

To a certain degree, the roots of the modern-day Hellenic armed forces can be traced back to September 1814, when the secretive *Philiki Etaireia* society was founded in Odesa; a group of Greeks with military experience that began plotting an uprising against the Ottoman rule and played an important role in the Greek War of Independence. Officially, at least the navy and army were established between 1821 and 1832. However, in the course of violent affairs that shook Greece over the following decades, each of the two was at least de facto disbanded, or suffered lengthy periods of decay, before being rebuilt in the early twentieth century and then involved in the previous-mentioned conflicts. Eventually, both were destroyed during the invasion of April 1941, and had to be almost completely rebuilt starting in 1944. Considering the heavy involvement of the officer corps in the politics and the poor economic state of the country, the Hellenic armed forces thus found little time for in-depth studies and innovation and were consistently dependent on foreign support for new equipment and knowledge.

Greece and NATO
Pending the Axis withdrawal from Greece of 1944, Greek politicians in exile met in Lebanon in May 1944, in attempt to organise a post-war order in the country. Between others, they agreed that all collaborationist forces would be prosecuted and punished, while all the resistance forces were to participate in the formation of the new armed forces. However, almost as soon as the British forces were in control of the country, their commander ordered a unilateral disarmament of the communist National Liberation Front (*Ethniko Apeleftherotiko Metopo*, EAM) and its military wing, the Greek People's Liberation Army (*Ellinikos Laikos Apeleftherotikos Stratos*, ELAS). At the same time, the British did nothing against the collaborationist Security Battalions (*Tagmafa Asfelaias*), formed to support the Axis occupation forces. In similar fashion, the British made no moves against members of the major anti-Nazi resistance group of the Second World War, the National Republican Greek League (*Ethnikos Dimokratikos Ellinikos Syndesmos-Ethnikes Omades Ellinon Antarton*, EDES-EOEA), although in February 1944, these reached a temporary agreement with the Germans to stop fighting each other and re-focus on countering the EAM-ELAS.

All the EAM ministers resigned in protest and a mass rally was organised in Athens on 3 December 1944, during which the Greek Police and Gendarmerie opened fire, killing 28 and wounding 148 protesters. Rather unsurprisingly, the EAM-ELAS refused to disarm and instead launched an armed insurgency; it simultaneously attempted to overthrow the government of Prime Minister Georgios Pandreou in Athens and attacked EDES positions in Epirus. While the EAM-ELAS secured most of the capital and the nearby port of Piraeus (the government was confined to the centre of Athens) and forced EDES to evacuate to Corfu, the British reacted with a military intervention. Apart from deploying the 3rd Greek Mountain Brigade, they flew in the 4th Indian Infantry Division from Italy. Ironically, except in Athens, the EAM-ELAS did not try to fight the British, but was foremost occupied with arresting Trotskyists, anarchists and other political dissidents.

In January 1945, the ELAS was forced to retreat from the city; its defeat also reduced the power of the EAM. However, this was only the beginning of the civil war that was to go on for four years. In fact, the open-ended commitment proved too much for Great Britain to bear and in 1947, the government in Athens began receiving active support from the USA, where the administration of the US President, Harry Truman defined a set of measures to prevent a communist take-over in Greece, Turkey and Iran (as the Truman Doctrine). The civil war ended with the military defeat of the communists; survivors were forced into exile and their organisations – foremost the Communist Party of Greece (*Kommounistiko Komma Elladas*, KKE) – were outlawed. Immediately afterwards, the Central Intelligence Agency of the USA (CIA), which already helped re-organise the Security Battalions into a secret society known as the IDEA (*Ieros Desmos Ellinon Axiomatikon*, or 'Holy Bond'), in cooperation with the Hellenic Armed Forces (*Ellinikes Enoples Dynamis*), led the country into the North Atlantic Treaty Organisation (NATO), in 1952.

Greece, a country considered a 'vital link' in the NATO's 'defence arc' spanning from the northernmost point in Norway to the eastern border of Iran, thus came under years of conservative rule, in which the governmental power was limited by the constitution and cautiously monitored by both the armed forces and the Hellenic National Intelligence Service (*Ethniki Ypiresia Pliroforion*, EYP), while any kind of leftist opposition was fiercely prosecuted.

M4 Sherman tanks of the British Army in front of the EAM building in downtown Athens, in December 1944. (Albert Grandolini Collection)

Hellenic Navy

Origins of the Hellenic Navy, the oldest branch of the nation's armed forces, can be traced to the early 1820s, when merchant fleet of Saronic islanders from Hydra, Spetsai and Poros, but also the islanders from Psara and Samos, began deploying their faster and more manoeuvrable fireships against the Ottoman supply vessels underway to the isolated garrisons. The resulting navy played a crucial role in the Greek War of Independence, through intercepting Ottoman supply vessels loaded with reinforcements and underway to quell the uprising. The combined Greek, British, French and Russian victory in the famous Battle of Navarino 1827, proved the key to achieving independence.

After the war, a Ministry of Naval Affairs was established under Admiral Konstantinos Kanaris, the Hellenic Navy established its headquarters in the port of Kapodistrias at the island of Poros and the service began working on improving the training of its officers. All progress was nullified during the tumults of 1831; indeed, even its brand-new flagship, frigate *Hellas* constructed in the USA, was torched by mutineers led by Admiral Andreas Miaoulis, while docked at Poros.

The re-building process was slow, gaining pace only in 1846, when a Naval School, commanded by Leonidas Palaskas, was founded on the corvette Loudovikos. Even then, there were constant tensions within the service – between those complaining about inefficient training and demanding modernisation and experienced but old-fashioned veterans of the war wanting independence. The result was an inefficient and poorly-organised service, limited to fighting piracy, monitoring the border and running transport operation. A new impetus was provided, starting in 1855, through the acquisition of the first propeller-driven ships with iron hulls, constructed in Great Britain: *Panopi*, *Plixavra*, *Afroessa*, and *Sfendoni*.

However, it was only in the 1880s that a French naval mission introduced a modern organisation, the methodological training of officers and enlisted personnel, and helped establish a training school. Unsurprisingly, the Royal Hellenic Navy was unable to realise any kind of achievements during the Cretan uprising of 1866. This failure prompted a fundamental re-think in regards of naval affairs. Over the following years, the service was expanded and bolstered through the acquisition of additional vessels with iron hulls, equipped with better guns and the first torpedoes. By the time of the Greco-Turkish War of 1897, the Hellenic Navy operated three new battleships constructed in France, but although establishing dominance in the Aegean Sea, these proved to have little influence for the developments on the land, where Greece lost severely.

In 1907, the Naval General Staff was established and the command of the navy assigned to Admiral Pavlos Kountouriotis. The service gradually came under the influence of a British Naval Mission, which led to the adoption of an English-style management, organisation, and training, and the acquisition of one armoured cruiser from Italy (named *Georgios Averof* in Greek service),

followed by two old battleships from the USA (USS *Mississippi*, BB-23, and USS *Idaho*, BB-24, which became *Kilkis* and *Lemnos*).

New vessels helped secure the Aegean Sea during the Balkan Wars but subsequently, the Hellenic Navy found itself confronted with a rapid growth of the competing Ottoman service. Due to the Greek reluctance to become involved in the First World War, much of the fleet was confiscated by the French and operated by them on convoy duties in the Aegean, until 1917. Over the following years, the reconstituted Royal Hellenic Navy took part in operations in the Aegean, where battleship *Averof* and its task force decimated the Ottoman fleet in the naval battles of Elli and Lemnos and helped liberate numerous islands. It went to support the White Armies in the Russian Civil War and took part in the Asia Minor Campaign.

During the 1920s, the navy sent *Averof* and *Elli* for repairs to France, acquired four torpedo boats in Great Britain, constructed new vessels at home and acquired six submarines from France. However, for most of the 1930s, spending for defence was greatly curtailed. It was only in 1938 that Athens placed an order for two modern destroyers, four minesweepers, a tanker and 12 hydroplanes in Great Britain. From that time onwards, coastal defences were organised into six districts, several minefields laid and protection of the most important naval facilities were bolstered through deployment of anti-aircraft artillery. The service entered the Second World War composed of two old battleships, one armoured cruiser, two light cruisers, 10 destroyers, and six submarines – but suffered an early loss when the cruiser *Elli* was sunk by the Italian submarine *Delfino* before the Italian invasion, while in the port of Tinos on 15 August 1940.

The Royal Hellenic Navy was decimated during the German invasion of 1941; both *Kilkis* and *Lemnos* were sunk by the Luftwaffe in the first days of the invasion, followed by 23 other vessels over the next three weeks. The surviving 17 warships – including six destroyers and five submarines –managed to reach the Souda Bay on Crete, before continuing to Egypt. However, most were found to be old and worn out and required overhauls and partial re-armament before being returned to service.

Rebuilt with warships of British and US origin, the Hellenic Navy took an active part in operations against Axis forces in the Mediterranean of 1943–1944 and two destroyers took part in the Operation Overlord (landings in Normandy of 1944). However, during the same year, the navy experienced a major setback during the Greek naval mutiny, which erupted on five warships in the port of Alexandria, in Egypt, over the composition of the Greek government-in-exile. The revolt was quickly quelled, but core reasons were not solved; they were to cause the civil war that erupted later the same year.

Greek battleship *Lemnos* (ex-USS *Idaho*, BB-24) at Constantinople in 1919. (USN photo)

A rare photograph showing Averoff together with the battleships *Kilkis* and *Lemnos*. The location is unknown, as is the exact date, which must be between 1927 and 1931, the year Kilkis was decommissioned. (Archive of the HNS Averoff)

During the conflict, the navy was forced to withdraw a number of obsolete vessels but was reinforced through the deliveries of one light cruiser as war reparations from Italy; 15 destroyers, destroyer escorts and frigates from the USA and Great Britain (six of which were returned to the Royal Navy between 1952 and 1960), and two diesel-electric-powered attack submarines from the US Navy. Once Greece joined NATO in 1952, the US and Greek navies ran numerous joint exercises and the US warships provided humanitarian relief to civilians following the earthquakes of 1953 and 1955. Indeed, with US help, the Greek Navy rebuilt its support fleet through the 1950s and by the end of the decade, this included two minelayers and 18 minehunters, 17 patrol boats and 15 other ships.

Except for minehunters – which played an important role in cleaning extensive minefields left over from the Second World War – another important type of warships during the 1940s and 1950s were amphibious warfare vessels. Initially, the fleet of these consisted of six British-made tank carriers (LST) and 12 landing craft (LCT) leased in 1945 and 1946. They were used for military and civilian transport due to the poor state of the Greek railway and road system. However, once the civil war was over, they proved surplus to requirements: four LCTs were returned to the UK in 1953 and all the others but two were sold in 1963. In similar fashion, all the LSTs were sold in the 1962–1964 period, without replacement.

Instead, as of 1963–1964, the navy operated a total of seven LST Mark 2s (*Chios*, L195; *Ikaria*, L154; *Lemnos*, L158; *Lesvos*, L172; *Rodos*, L157; *Samos*, L179, and *Syros*, L144), donated by or leased from the USA in the period 1943–1964. With a maximum speed of only 10 knots (19km/h), these were slow vessels. However, they were 116 metres long and displaced 4,877 tons, armed with one twin gun 40mm calibre and six automatic cannon 20mm calibre, could load up to 18 tanks or 33 trucks and had berths for 217 troops.

Finally, between 1959 and 1962, the Hellenic Navy was significantly reinforced through the transfer of six *Fletcher*-class destroyers leased from the reserves of the US Navy. Constructed in large numbers (175 hulls) between 1942 and 1944, this was a highly successful design, which also proved popular in service. Fletchers had a high maximum speed of 38 knots (70km/h) and principal armament of five guns 127mm (5-in) calibre. Their heavy torpedo armament was removed and replaced by additional anti-aircraft guns 20 and 40mm calibre, but they initially retained their two depth charge tracks.

Table 1: Major Warships of the Royal Hellenic Navy, 1963–1964

Hull Number	Name	Type	Origin
24	Elli	gun cruiser	ex-*Eugenio di Savoia* (Italy)
01	Aetos	destroyer	ex-*Slater* (DE-766; USA)
02	Adrias	"	ex-*Tanatside* (L69; UK)
03	Aigaion	"	ex-*Lauderdale* (L95; UK)
06	Aspis	"	ex-*Conner* (DD-582; USA)
10	Kanaris	"	ex-*Hatherleigh* (L53; UK)
15	Hastings	"	ex-*Catterick* (L81; UK)
16	Velos	"	ex-*Charrette* (DD-581; USA)
20	Doxa	"	ex-*Ludlow* (DD-438; USA)
28	Thyella	"	ex-*Bradford* (DD-545; USA)
29	Themistocles	"	ex-*Bramham* (L51; UK)
31	Ierax	"	ex-*Ebert* (DE-768; USA)
54	Leon	"	ex-*Eldridge* (DE-173; USA)
56	Lonchi	"	ex-*Hall* (DD-583; USA)
63	Navainon	"	ex-*Brown* (DD-546; USA)
65	Niki	"	ex-*Eberle* (DD-430; USA)
67	Panthir	"	ex-*Garfield Thomas* (DE-193; USA)
85	Sfendoni	"	ex-*Aulick* (DD-569; USA)
78	Poseidon	attack submarine	ex-*Lapon* (SS-260; USA)
17	Amphitriti	"	ex-*Jack* (SS-259; USA)

The cruiser *Elli*, constructed in Italy 1935, displaced 8,850 tons and was armed with eight guns 152mm calibre and six of 100mm calibre, eight anti-aircraft guns 37mm calibre and 12 of 20mm calibre, six torpedo tubes 533mm calibre and depth charges. The ship had 40–100mm armour and could accelerate to 36 knots. (Tom Cooper collection)

MODIFIED GATOS

The most important submarines operated by the Greek and Turkish navies of the 1960s were *Gato*-class vessels of US origin. Originally, this series of 77 was constructed for the US Navy between 1941 and 1944 and armed with 10 torpedo tubes 533mm calibre (21in; with storage capacity of 24 torpedoes), one deck gun 76mm calibre and a single each 40mm Bofors and 20mm Oerlikon gun. They were large boats; 95m long and displacing 2,424 tons when submerged, designed for 75-days-long patrols from Hawaii to Japan. This was necessary to provide them not only with a top range of 20,000km (11,000 nautical miles), but also to provide the crew with the comfort necessary for operations in tropical conditions.

Correspondingly – though entirely unusually for their time – they included separate bunks for almost every crew member, showers, air conditioning, refrigerated storage for food and freshwater distilling units. Some 57 have survived the Second World War: seven were re-configured into the so-called 'hunter-killer' configuration, as submarines equipped to hunt other submarines. They were comprehensively silenced, received a streamlined GUPPY-type of sail (GUPPY stood for Greater Underwater Propulsion Power Programme) with a snorkel, and advanced sonars. However, they were quickly surpassed by nuclear-powered SSNs, and decommissioned starting in 1959. Instead, the large fleet of relatively new and modern boats was offered to Allied foreign navies. Italy received two, Japan one, Brazil two, while Greece received two. The latter have received only partial streamlining to the fairwater and snorkels, but they originally retained their 76mm deck guns.

The Greek Navy submarine *Poseidon* (hull number S-78), of the Gato-class, as seen in 1961. Like the other Greek vessel of this class – *Amphitriti* – she became involved in clandestine operations around Cyprus of the 1960s, the mass of which remains obscure. (USN photo)

Hellenic Army of the 1960s

Officially established in 1828, the Hellenic Army was – nominally – the second oldest, yet the largest branch of the Greek armed forces of the 1960s and one with more than a century of operational history. Strongly influenced – in tactics and appearance – by the French Colonel Charles Gavier during its first years of existence, it grew rapidly until 1831, when it all but ceased to exist amid internal political turmoil. Consequently, the Bavarian prince Otto initially relied on a 4,000-strong German contingent, until a new regular army was re-established which by 1860, counted up to 200,000.

Through the 1870s, a new French military mission was invited, which helped reform the force, re-organise it into divisions and brigades and emboldened Athens into sending cadets abroad for education. Even so, the branch performed dismally during the Greco-Turkish War of 1897, when the Ottomans pushed the Greeks out of Thessaly. Athens reacted with another reform, once again under French supervision. Between others, this reorganised the mobilisation system and adopted the 'triade' organisation, along which three platoons were organised into a company, three companies into a battalion, three battalions into a regiment, and three regiments into a division. The resulting army fought skilfully during the Balkan Wars, enabling the country to double its territory.

Greece's participation in the First World War remained limited and was followed by the disastrous experiences in Turkey of 1919–1922, including the mass flight of both the Greek Army and the Greek population from the Anatolian Peninsula. After a period of stagnation and another reform, the Hellenic Army successfully pushed back the Italian invasion of October 1940 and occupied large parts of southern Albania, but proved no match for the Wehrmacht of April 1941. Still, significant parts managed to evacuate to the Middle East, while minor units escaped into the mountains, where they continued the war on the Allied side under the exiled Greek government. Mid-through its post-war re-establishment, the army was embroiled in the five-years-long civil war, which left the country devastated.

In 1947, the faltering British military and economic assistance was replaced by a US intervention: thanks to the US-administered Marshal Plan, Greece not only received a total of US$200 million in immediate economic assistance, in 1950, but also 1.7 billion in military assistance. The country experienced rapid economic recovery and in 1952, joined NATO, which considered (and still considers) it a fundamental link in its defences of southern and south-eastern Europe.

Meanwhile, Athens drafted an ambitious plan for deployment of an entire brigade on the side of the United Nations (UN) in Korea, but in the aftermath of victories against the North Korean invasion of autumn 1950, reduced its participation to a unit known as the Sparta Battalion. Commanded by Lieutenant-Colonel Georgios Koumanakos, this 849-strong unit drawn from the 1st, 8th and 9th Infantry Division arrived at Pusan on 9 December 1950. It comprised three rifle companies (each with the headquarters platoon, one machine gun and mortar platoon and three rifle platoons). Effective from 23 August 1953, it was expanded to 1,063 troops, and maintained at that level until December 1953: subsequently, the battalion was further enlarged to a brigade-sized unit of 2,163. Recruited on the basis of their proficiency in English language, Greeks serving in Korea brought with them combat experience from the Greek Civil War and familiarity with US-made weaponry and equipment. One of companies participated in the defence of the Outpost Harry, earning itself the Presidential Unit Citation, while individual officers and other ranks were honoured with six Distinguished Service Crosses, 32 Silver Stars, and 110 Bronze Stars for their bravery.

Eventually, 10,255 Greek military personnel served in Korea, of whom 186 or 187 were killed (all bodies were repatriated) and 617 wounded. This participation was brought to an end by the anti-Greek riots in Istanbul of September 1955, which suddenly soured not only relations between Athens and Ankara, but also with NATO; by December 1955, only 191 Greek Army troops were left in South Korea.

Meanwhile, Athens began receiving extensive financial and military aid, enabling an expansion of its military into one of largest conventional forces in Europe (relative to the country's size and population). By the 1960s, the Hellenic Army was organised into three corps, including 11 infantry divisions, one armoured division, one commando brigade, two battalions equipped with US-made, MGR-1 Honest John nuclear-capable, surface-to-surface rockets, and one with US-made MIM-23 HAWK surface-to-air missiles (SAMs). It was equipped with about 200 M47 Patton main battle tanks (MBTs); was in the process of receiving improved M48 tanks; had about 50 US-made M24 and M41 light tanks and a sizeable amount of artillery pieces 105, 155, 175 and 203mm calibre, as well as anti-aircraft artillery 40, 75 and 90mm calibre. The majority of its 100,000 of peace-time personnel were conscripts, drafted from all able-bodied men between the ages of 21 and 50, and serving 24 months.

The Royal Hellenic Air Force

The Greek Army was among the first to recognise the importance of air power and start deploying aircraft for offensive purposes. In 1911, Athens contracted a group of French aviators to help create a flying service. Six army officers were sent to the Henry Farman Flight School outside Paris and an order for Farman and Nieuport aircraft was placed. Following their return, the delivery of the aircraft and their assembly, on 8 February 1912, Emanuel Argyropoulos became the first Greek pilot to make a manned flight on a powered aircraft in Greece. He took off in one of the Nieuports from an aerodrome near Athens, and in presence of the King and his government, dozens of officers and a large crowd of civilians, made a circle over Rouf and Thisseio, before landing safely, some 16 minutes later.

The first official unit, the 'Air Company', was established at Larissa in September 1912; it included four Farman aeroplanes, four pilots, one French engineer, a few technicians and 50 other soldiers. At that time, the Greeks took care to arm their aircraft by bombs manufactured by the Matsinotis factory in Athens: these weighed 1kg, had cylindrical bodies with spherical ending and a contact fuse. The unit saw deployment for observation purposes during the First Balkan War of 1912–1913. Before soon, one of the Greek Farman's was armed and except for flying reconnaissance missions for the navy, bombarded the Turkish fleet in the Dardanelles with four hand grenades in the course of the first naval-warfare-support mission ever flown.

Meanwhile, early in 1914, with support of the British Naval Mission, the Hellenic Navy followed with the establishment of its own naval aviation service. Based at Phaleron, this was equipped with Farman and Sopwith seaplanes operated by Greek officers. However, while Athens then placed an order for Sopwith Gun Bus twin-float seaplanes from Great Britain, only a few were delivered: the majority were commandeered by the Royal Naval Air Service (the contemporary air arm of the Royal Navy) at the outbreak of the First World War.

Troubles over whether Greece should join the First World War or not and on which side, then resulted in a period during which further growth of the nascent flying branch became extremely difficult. It was only once all flying units had joined the Venizelos government in Thessaloniki, in September 1916, that they were rebuilt with help of Greek officers and non-commissioned officers (NCOs) trained as pilots and mechanics at schools operated by the French in Thessaloniki, and by the British at Moudros, on the island of Limnos. The result was the Hellenic Air Service, which was split into two sections. One operated in support of French-commanded forces in Macedonia, while the other operated with the British forces in the Mediterranean.

Meanwhile, additional Greek airmen were trained in Britain and France; some were subsequently distributed to Allied air forces, while others formed the personnel of three units of what by 1918, was the Royal Hellenic Army Air Service: No. 531 Fighter, No 532 Bomber, and No. 533 Reconnaissance Squadrons. Around the same time, the Royal Hellenic Naval Air Service was reorganised into four units: H1, H2, H3, and H4.

Both flying branches continued to grow through the 1920s, when Athens bought numerous surplus aircraft from the Allies. By 1921, the naval service – home-based at Phaleron and trained by a British Naval Mission – included 70 pilots flying de Havilland DH.4s and DH.9s, Sopwith Camels and Short 184 reconnaissance-bombers. Meanwhile, the Royal Hellenic Army Air Force grew to about 100 pilots, flying Breguet 14A-2s and B-2s, Spad S-7C.1s and Nieuport 28-C.1s from bases at Goudi, near Athens, from Drama and Thessaloniki. The latter service deployed three mixed units during what the Greeks called the 'Asia Minor Campaign' (the Turkish War of Independence) and they quickly established complete air superiority over the western Anatolian Peninsula. However, intensive utilisation of aircraft, denial of logistic support by the British and French and developments on the ground, rendered this force ineffective by September 1922.

What was left of the two flying branches was completely reorganised once a republic was proclaimed in 1924 and re-equipped with 25 Gloster Mars VI Nighthawk fighters. However, subsequently – and although the government in Athens agreed with the top brass of the armed forces that there was a necessity to develop a powerful air force – this proved unable to support a further build-up. The situation was saved by voluntary subscriptions from civilians. The municipality of Kavala alone collected enough funds for five new aircraft, while others provided for another 15. Thus, by 1926 – when also the first locally-manufactured aircraft, a Blakburn Velos seaplane, was assembled by the State Aircraft Factory – the Hellenic Army Air Force was back to around 75 pilots organised into two squadrons, home-based at Goudi and Drama.

Meanwhile, the Hellenic Naval Air Service acquired several Avro 504N trainers and was operating these from training schools at Tatoi and Phaleron. By the late 1920s, the army air force was expanded to three squadrons flying Breguet 19A-2s/B-2s, and Morane-Saulnier MS.147s, and the naval air service acquired Hawker Horsley torpedo-bombers from Great Britain. Correspondingly, in May 1931, Athens made the decision to amalgamate the two into the Hellenic Air Force (*Polemiki Aeroporia*, PA), as an independent branch of the armed forces under the control of Air Ministry. Following necessary re-organisation, the service was organised into a section responsible for supporting the army, consisting of three mixed squadrons (No. 1 at Tatoi, No. 2 at Larissa, and No. 3 at Sedes), and three flying schools. The section supporting the navy had two flights based at Phaleron and one torpedo-bombing flight and a flying school at Tatoi, which was particularly well-equipped, and included a technical school and a General Training and Trades School.

With the restoration of the monarchy of 1934, the service was re-designated the Royal Hellenic Air Force (RHAF; *Elliniki Vasiliki Aeroporia*) and re-equipped again. By the time of the Italian invasion in 1940, it acquired 36 Polish-made PZL P-24F and nine Bloch MB.151 fighters for three squadrons; enough Fairey Battle and Potez 63s for two squadrons; while Henschel Hs.126 army cooperation monoplanes were operated by one unit. The naval cooperation squadron flew 10 Avro Anson Mk I reconnaissance-bombers, 10 Dornier Do.22s, and nine Fairey IIIF floatplanes. Finally, two Gloster Gladiator fighters were sponsored by Stylianos Sarpakis, a Greek-Egyptian businessman.

Although lacking logistic support and poorly trained, the morale of Greek pilots was high and they managed to destroy numerous aircraft of the much larger Regia Aeronautica (Italian Air Force), both in the sky and on the ground. Indeed, Greek bomber squadrons flew repeated air strikes on Italian supply lines in Albania and air bases of Corytsa and Agyrocastro. That said, losses were heavy; trained personnel was lost in action faster than could be replaced and thus, London eventually ordered the deployment of RAF fighter squadrons operating Gladiators (replaced by Hawker Hurricanes in early 1941), and a donation of additional Gladiators to Greece.

The relief provided in this fashion proved rather short by nature; on 6 April 1941, Nazi Germany invaded and – supported by about 400 combat aircraft based in Bulgaria – quickly overwhelmed the Greek armed forces. By 23 April, the British withdrew from the country, together with enough aircraft and personnel of the RHAF to form the nucleus of a new air arm. In 1942, the British helped establish its first new unit, No. 335 (Fighter) Squadron, equipped with Hawker Hurricane Mk IIs, in Egypt. The second unit, No. 336, followed in February 1943. Both saw action in the Western Desert before being re-equipped with Supermarine Spitfires and deployed for operations against Axis forces in Greece. The latter became the primary mission of No. 13 (Light Bomber) Squadron, equipped with Avro Ansons and later on, with Bristol Blenheim Mk IVs and Mk Vs, which also undertook anti-submarine patrols. In 1944, No. 13 Squadron – meanwhile re-equipped with Martin Baltimores – joined the RAF Balkan Air Force and began flying interdiction strikes on enemy communications in Yugoslavia.

Following the liberation of Greece, Nos. 13, 335 and 336 Squadrons were repatriated to Greece, where they took part in operations against several islands still controlled by German garrisons, before being passed under Greek control, on 25 April 1946. Almost immediately, the two fighter units – which meanwhile flew Supermarine Spitfire F.Mk IXs – were pressed into combat against the communist guerrillas in the north of the country. In 1947, they were reinforced by the delivery of additional Spitfire F.Mk IXe/XVIs, which enabled the establishment of a third unit, No. 337 Squadron (or 'Mira', in local parlance). Moreover, the USA provided North American T-6 Texan advanced trainers and light strikers and Douglas C-47 Dakota transports.

However, attempts to expand the RHAF were greatly slowed down by the lack of necessary funding and equipment; even the majority of air bases was systematically destroyed by the retreating German forces. Athens eventually managed to acquire only surplus Curtiss SB2C-4 Helldiver dive-bombers, which entered service with 336 Squadron, and proved their worth in strikes against fortified insurgent positions in mountainous areas. By the time the communists were suppressed in summer 1949, the air force was reinforced through a few Stinson L-5 liaison and observation aircraft and some of its C-47s were modified to carry bombs. However, most of remaining aircraft were badly worn out. Thus, and just like the army and navy, the RHAF experienced a true 'new start' once Greece joined NATO.

Three young lieutenants of the RHAF, as seen in front of one of Spitfire F.Mk IXs they flew from Sedes AB, in 1950. (Vassilios Trakas Collection)

RHAF IN KOREA

Perhaps the least-well-known operation of the RHAF was its involvement in the Korean War. On 11 November 1950, a squadron of seven C-47s of the 355 Transport Squadron (comprising 67 officers and other ranks) embarked a ship that brought them to Japan arriving on 1 December 1950. Once in theatre, they were assigned to the 21st Troop Carrier Squadron, US Air Force (USAF). Later on, the unit was re-designated the 6461st Troop Carrier Squadron and assigned to the 374th Wing, USAF. Initially based at Taegu AB, the unit played a crucial role in supporting US troops during the Battle of Chosin Reservoir. On

14 May 1951, it was re-located to Kimpo AB, where it remained until 23 May 1955. Throughout its involvement, tasks of the Greek transport squadron included transport of personnel and supplies, evacuations and ammunition drops. In total, it carried out impressive 70,568 passengers, including 9,243 wounded, and logged 13,777 flight hours. In turn, it lost 12 officers and other ranks and two C-47s, but earned itself the Presidential Unit Citation for playing a pivotal role in evacuating US Marines from Hagaru-ri, in December 1950 (each crewmember involved was also decorated by the Air Medal).

28th Tactical Air Command

Meanwhile, aiming to quickly integrate the RHAF into its command structure, NATO first ensured hundreds of pilots and technicians underwent training by USAF instructors. A comprehensive air base construction programme was initiated, resulting in emergence of about a dozen modern air bases outside Larissa, Eleusis, Souda, Nea Anchialos, Tatoi, Tanagra and Peloponnesus, all connected by fuel pipelines. A chain of nine, early warning radar stations was constructed, several of these high in the Pindus mountains.

This infra-structure was used to support deliveries of 82 Canadair Sabre F.Mk 2 and F.Mk 4s interceptors, about 250 Republic F-84G Thunderjet fighter-bombers, Lockheed T-33A jet trainers and Sikorsky H-19 Chickasaw helicopters. Moreover, the RHAF received additional C-47s – which were used to re-activate the 13th Mira. The main reception base for all this equipment was

Eleusis AB and the locally-based, 112th Wing. Standard practice saw the reception of the new aircraft, training of core personnel and the work-up of operational units, which were then distributed to their new home-bases. It was in this fashion that a reconnaissance component also came into being in 1952, when the 335th Tactical Reconnaissance Squadron was established to fly F-84Gs modified through the installation of two K24 cameras into the tip of their port drop tank.

Overall, the force was organised into four combat wings (of which three were equipped with F-84Gs, and one with Sabres) and 10 squadrons, officially assigned to NATO as the 28th Tactical Air Command. Its operations were supported by the 30th Air Material Command, while the flight school was expanded into an Air Force Academy with a three-year course, a Reserve Training Centre, an Aircrew Centre and an Engineering School, all controlled by the 31st Air Training Command.

The build-up was still incomplete when Athens and NATO agreed to start upgrading the air force. This resulted in a series of unit-re-organisations and re-deployments that went on for years. In August 1956, the 348th Squadron ('Mira' in local parlance) became one of first European units equipped with Republic RF-84F Thunderflash reconnaissance fighters. About a year later, the RHAF received its first Republic F-84F Thunderstreak fighter-bombers: their deliveries were to last until 1962, by when 75 aircraft from surplus stocks of the USAF are known to have been handed over. Additional F-84Fs were subsequently donated by Germany and the Netherlands.

The first unit operating Thunderstreaks became the 335th Mira, which as of 1957, was based at Larissa and in Tanagra from 1960. It continued operating this type until May 1965, when it was re-equipped with F-104Gs. The 336th Mira followed in March 1959, while assigned to the 111th Wing and based at Nea Anchialos; in December 1962, this unit served as the founding squadron of the newly-established 116th Wing, home-based at Araxos, and began converting to F-104Gs in 1965. In August 1959, the 339th Squadron – established in 1952 to fly F-84Gs – converted to F-84Fs and moved

to Larissa: in April 1960, it re-deployed to Nea Anchialos, where it was re-assigned to the 111th Wing.

Another Thunderjet unit, the 340th Squadron, began receiving F-84Fs in early 1960, while based at Nea Anchialos and assigned to the 111th Wing: however, only months later, this was re-deployed to the 115th Wing as Souda. Sabre-equipped units followed in fashion. The 342nd Squadron – established in 1953 – was re-equipped with F-84Fs in 1965, while assigned to the 111th Wing at Nea Anchialos: it continued flying Thunderstreaks until 1969, when these were replaced by Convair F-102 Delta Daggers, this time flying from 114th Wing in Tanagra. However, its F-84Fs, along with some of the pilots, were incorporated in a new Squadron, namely the 344th Mira, operating from 110th Wing in Larissa.

Finally, in January 1965, the 336th Squadron began converting to F-104Gs. One more squadron, the 349th Mira founded in 1967 flew the Thunderstreak from 110th Wing in Larissa, probably equipped with the 336th Mira fighter-bombers and a core of its personnel and three years later, transferred to the 111th Wing and re-equipped with F/RF-5A/Bs in 1970.

Above: A Canadair Sabre F.Mk 2 or F.Mk 4 (Canadian-made F-86E/F Sabre) of the RHAF rolling for take-off, in the mid-1950s. (PA)

Below: An elevated view of the top side of an F-84G Thunderjet of the RHAF. No less than 250 such fighter jets were delivered by USA in the 1950s. (PA)

A nice study of an F-84G Thunderjet of the RHAF, as seen with large parts of the fin and wing-tip fuel tanks painted in red, for exercise purposes, in the late 1950s. (PA)

Sabre Dogs, Starfighters and Freedom Fighters

Apart from receiving a large number of fighter-bombers, the RHAF was equipped with a strong air defence component. In 1956, the 114th Wing came into being. This included 341st, 342nd and 343rd Miras, all equipped with North American F-86E Sabre jet interceptors. A few years later, the Air Defence Command (ADC) of the USAF – a branch responsible for aerial defence of continental USA – began introducing into service the Convair's brand-new interceptor: F-102A Delta Dart. With the ADC still having significant numbers of relatively new North American F-86D Sabre Dogs in service, the decision was taken to overhaul 35 of these at the Societa per Aviazioni Fiat, in Italy, before handing them over to the RHAF.

Greek pilots found it easy to adapt to the new type as many of them had already flown the Canadair-made Sabres. However, the equipment and armament of the F-86Ds were unusual. This version was designed as an all-weather interceptor; although equipped with the AN/APG-36 radar installed inside a radome above the intake, it was meant to be operated under a tight ground control. Furthermore, it had no machine guns or cannon armament installed: instead, it received a retractable launcher for 24 Mk 4 Mighty Mouse unguided rockets 70mm calibre. While these were considered an excellent weapon for attacks on slow and heavy bombers, they were almost useless in air combat against jet fighters. The solution was found in the installation of GAR-8 Sidewinder, infra-red homing air-to-air missiles (in September 1962, in the process of simplification of all the US military designations, the GAR-8 was re-designated as the AIM-9B Sidewinder). Eventually, the RHAF established two units equipped with F-86Ds: the 337 Squadron, home-based at Eleusis and assigned to the 112th Wing, and later on, 343rd Mira, home-based at Nea Anchialos, and assigned to the 111th Wing.

Meanwhile, the build-up of the air defence component went on through the service entry of the MIM-14 Nike Hercules medium and high-altitude SAMs. From May 1960, these were operated by the 350th 'Squadron' (which actually consisted of four squadron-sized units) and protected Athens.

Sabre Dogs and Nike Hercules had hardly been in service when in 1961, the Pentagon decided to supply 35 Canadair-built F-104G Starfighters within the Mutual Assistance Programme – and then as nuclear-armed strike fighters. Eventually, the RHAF received not only these, but also a mix of four Lockheed-made TF-104Gs and 10 F-104Gs, and two TF-104Gs from USAF stocks. Beginning in 1965, they equipped the 335th Mira of the 114th Wing at the newly-constructed Tanagra AB and the 336th Mira of the 116th Wing at Araxos, although the conversion of the second unit lasted well into 1966.

Finally, in 1965, Greece was one of the first customers for the then, brand-new Northrop F-5A/B Freedom Fighter, a light-weight supersonic fighter-bomber, developed specifically with simplicity of maintenance and operations with poorer Western Allies in mind. The initial order was for 80 aircraft, meant to equip two wings; 341st Mira of the 111th Wing was the first to convert to the new type and it was declared operational on 15 July 1965. The following year, 343rd Mira of the 113th Wing followed, but the planned third squadron – the 349th – was only partially re-equipped when relations to the USA suddenly deteriorated due to political developments in Athens.

Overall, as of 1963–1967, the RHAF boasted the strength of about 17,800 officers and other ranks – including some 350 pilots – and 300 aircraft and helicopters, organised as listed in Table 2.

Table 2: Major Units of the RHAF, 1963–1967

Wing	Squadron	Base	Aircraft Type & Notes
110th Wing	349 Mira	Larissa	(est.1967) F-84F
111th Wing	339 Mira	Nea Anchialos	F-84F
	341 Mira	"	F-86E(M)/CL-13 Sabre F.Mk 2 (to F-5A in 1965)
	342 Mira	"	F-86E(M)/CL-13 Sabre F.Mk 2 (to F-84F in 1964)
	343 Mira	Nea Anchialos	F-86D & T-33A/CT-133 (to F-5A in 1966)
112th Wing	337 Mira	Eleusis	F-86D (to F-5A in 1967, then re-assigned to 111th Wing)
	361 Mira	"	T-33A & T-37A (to 111th Wing in 1963–1964, then 120th Wing at Kalamata AB)
	355 Mira	"	C-47
113th Wing	356 Mira	Sedes Salonica	C-47
114th Wing	335 Mira	Tanagra	F-84F (to F-104G in 1964–1965)
115th Wing	338 Mira	Souda	F-84G (to F-84F in 1964)
	340 Mira	Souda	F-84F (reorganised as 338 Mira in 1964)
116th Wing	336 Mira	Araxos	F-84F (to F-104G in 1964–1965)
Niki Wing	350 Mira	Athens	4 Flights of MIM-14 SAMs

THE COLD WAR WARHORSE

An F-84F Thunderstreak of the RHAF, as seen relatively shortly after delivery, which began in 1958. (PA)

Nowadays largely forgotten, at least overshadowed by recollections about the Republic F-84 Thunderjet, for many of air forces of European NATO members, the F-84F Thunderstreak and the RF-84F Thunderflash were true 'warhorses' of the first 'hot' phase of the Cold War: the period of the late 1950s and early 1960s, that peaked with the Berlin Wall Crisis and then the Cuban Missile Crisis. At the first look, alone the nomenclature of these jets is confusing, because the well-known F-84A/B/C/D/E and F-84G variants, which belonged to what some perceive as the '1st generation of jet fighters' and saw intensive combat service during the Korean War, were all straight-wing models called the Thunderjet, while – although their design was originally based on that of earlier variants – the F-84F and RF-84F were actually entirely different aircraft with swept wings. Both came into being in the late 1940s, when Republic's designers attempted to put swept wings on the original F-84 design in hope to match performances of the North American F-86 Sabre. Simultaneously, the USAF was searching for a high-performance interceptor powered by the British Armstrong Siddeley Sapphire turbojet built by Wright as J65. While sound, this idea quickly ran into problems, resulting in massive delays in production and an underperforming jet, suffering from engine-related problems, prone to stall pitch-up, irrecoverable when spinning, and having a poor turning ability at combat speeds. Although problems were gradually solved, and USAF eventually placed orders for no less than 3,428, the type was soon replaced by North American F-100 Super Sabre.

Thus, huge numbers of F-84Fs were supplied to nine NATO air forces in Europe, all of which were in urgent need of jet fighters to bolster their numbers at the time both the East and the West were rapidly re-arming. This even more so because Thunderstreaks came with the capability to deploy nuclear weapons from the US arsenal and were thus offering the nuclear option to the countries that had none of its own 'bombs'.

Something similar was valid for RF-84Fs: the reconnaissance version emerged as a result of an attempt to improve the performance through installing intakes in the wing-roots. The idea did not work, but this arrangement resulted in a jet with a nose big enough for up to 15 sophisticated and reliable reconnaissance cameras – in addition to retaining the combat capability in the form of four internally installed machine guns and underwing stores. The RF-84Fs were some of most advanced tactical reconnaissance jets of their time, including many 'firsts'. They were equipped with TriMetrogen cameras and a computerised control system that calculated the speed, altitude and the light, to adjust settings of every camera optimally, resulting in photographs with higher delineation. They were also equipped with a vertical viewfinder; essentially a periscope installed to the cockpit panel which showed the pilot the terrain below. Finally, each received a cockpit voice recorder enabling pilots to make 'mental notes' during the mission, adding details that might not appear on photographs. Unsurprisingly, RF-84Fs saw long and distinguished service with many of European air forces, but especially in Greece and Turkey, where the last examples remained in service well into the 1980s.

An RF-84F Thunderflash reconnaissance jet of the RHAF in flight over central Greece of the late 1950s. Interestingly, the Greek air force began receiving this variant even before F-84F fighter-bombers, in 1957. (PA)

The North American F-86D Sabre was the first radar-equipped interceptor of the RHAF. Rather surprisingly for its pilots, it came equipped with GAR-8/AIM-9 Sidewinder missiles and unguided rockets – although without any machine guns or cannons. (PA)

The Lockheed F-104G Starfighter was to mark the beginning of a new era for the RHAF; 35 were provided to Greece within the MAP, to serve as nuclear strike fighters. At the time the Cyprus Crisis erupted in late 1963, two units were in the process of conversion to the type and thus saw no action over the island. (PA)

3
TURKISH ARMED FORCES OF THE MID-1960s

Like the Greek forces, so also could the Turkish Armed Forces of the mid-1960s look back at a rich military history but had relatively little recent combat experience. While reforms of the Ottoman armed forces in the mid-nineteenth century were primarily influenced by French advisors, starting in 1880, a German military advisory team led by Lieutenant-Colonel Otto Köhler arrived in Istanbul. There followed a period of close cooperation between Berlin and Istanbul that was particularly intensified once General Colmar Freiherr von der Goltz – famous as the top military historian and theoretician – was contracted in 1896. Goltz's ideology of a strong, authoritarian and militant 'nation in arms' influenced the last generation of Ottoman military officers (and thus many of the Young Turks,

including Atatürk) and also the leaders of the Turkish Armed Forces (Türk Silahli Kuvvetleri; TSK), following the creation of the Turkish Republic. One of reasons being that it prompted a rapid growth of the military educational system, which produced a highly educated, self-conscious corps of a meritocratic and cosmopolitan elite, efficient in commanding armed forces during the First World War and the Turkish War of Independence, but also excelling in law and in international and domestic business and administration.

Ottoman relations with the German Empire were far from one-sided; they resembled a partnership. Von der Goltz was influential in the emergence of many of Ottoman military theoreticians, perhaps the most famous of whom was the Baghdad-born, Mahmoud

Sheyket. Amongst others, Sheyket published two tactical manuals and his and Goltz's military thoughts became the basic textbook for Atatürk and allies when they were forming the Turkish Republic. It was for this mixture of reasons that not only the Ottoman Army became one of the first, world-wide, to adapt the 'triade' organisational pattern, but was also one of the first to establish what is nowadays colloquially known as 'special forces'.

The experiences from the Tripolitania and especially in Macedonia from the Balkan Wars, prompted its General Staff to establish the Special Organisation, in 1913. This was designed to function as an intelligence-gathering and counterespionage service at home and abroad, with a secondary task of instigating insurgencies on territories lost to enemies. Headquartered in Istanbul, it was organised into four departments, including the European Section, the Caucasian Section, the Africa and Libya Section and the Eastern Province Section. True scope of its activities during the Turkish War of Independence remain unclear, but it remains in existence – in a different form – to this very day.

Decades of Neutrality

Early through its existence, the Republic of Turkey had faced several rebellions that required military action. For example, the Kurds in south-eastern Anatolia, who constituted around 20 percent of the country's population, revolted several times between 1925 and 1929 and again, in 1937–1939 during the infamous Dersim rebellion. However, in military terms, these were little more than police actions, which, while violent, did not add much to the warfighting experience. During the first half of the 1940s, at least the army and air force received significant Allied and some German equipment and training (but not the navy). However, the infantry in particular, struggled to assimilate modern equipment and tactics and there was no substitute for combat experience.[1] Foremost, officer promotion was almost always by seniority, which led to over-staffed senior ranks with virtually no experience in modern warfare.

This system suppressed the rise of competitors, while securing the loyalty of the Turkish Armed Forces. Ironically, while Atatürk strictly prohibited any kind of political activities by officers in active service, the TSK was indoctrinated to perceive itself as the guardian of the Kemalism and especially its secular aspects. Correspondingly, its General Staff continued maintaining an important degree of influence over the decision-making processes in Ankara, especially in regards of national security – even before Mustafa Kemal Atatürk's death in 1938. Another irony related to Atatürk is that despite his radical secular reforms, he remained highly popular in the Muslim world – principally because he was (and remains) remembered for defeating Western Imperialism. Unsurprisingly, Mustafa Ismet Inönü (former officer of the Ottoman Army and prime minister under Atatürk from 1923 until 1937, and again in 1961–1964), the country's second president, kept the country out of the Second World War.

Although the TSK was mobilised, it saw no combat other than occasional border skirmishing. Turkey did declare war on Axis powers in February 1945, but although there was a plan to send two divisions to Italy, the conflict was over before these could be deployed.

After the Second World War, faithful to Kemalist ideology that desired to develop a parliamentary democracy, Inönü allowed Turkey's first multi-party elections to be held in 1946. However, these proved neither free nor fair and – amid widespread anti-Communist hysteria – the president was forced to intervene through banning all the leftist parties. A new attempt was launched in form of national elections in 1950, when Inönü's Republican Party was promptly defeated by the Democratic Party. However, the transfer of power to the government of Bayar and Adnan Menderes was peaceful.

One of ironies about the nascent Turkish Republic is that much of military success of the forces under Atatürk's command became possible due to supplies of gold, arms and ammunition from the nascent Soviet Union. Turkey continued purchasing Soviet armament during the 1930s, like this T-26 tank. (Albert Grandolini Collection)

Above: During the Second World War, Turkey found itself in a unique position to purchase arms from very different sources. This included PZL 24 fighters of Polish design and manufacture, like this example. (Albert Grandolini Collection)

Left: …and also Spitfires (foreground) of British and Focke Wulf 190s of German origins. (Albert Grandolini Collection)

Korean War

On Sunday 25 June 1950, North Korean forces invaded South Korea. Many Soviet-equipped North Korean troops were veterans of the Red Army that defeated the Japanese at the close of the Second World War and the subsequent Chinese Civil War. The South Korean Army (ROK) comprised lightly equipped raw troops and the US contingent had been reduced to a regimental combat team of advisors. The United Nations condemned the aggression and on 7 July, appointed General Douglas MacArthur to command UN forces being sent to save South Korea. The North Korean troops overwhelmed the US and ROK units until a defensive line was established around the port of Pusan in south-eastern Korea. British troops arrived on 28 August, the first of many national contingents and the perimeter held against sustained North Korean attacks on a broad front. On 15 September, a US amphibious force landed at Inchon, recapturing the South Korean capital Seoul 11 days later. By 30 September,

North Korean troops had crossed the border back to North Korea. The UN then mandated an invasion of North Korea, which led to North Korean forces being pushed back to the Chinese border. This resulted in China intervening in the war, eventually driving UN forces back to their positions along the 38th Parallel. This ended the mobile phase of the war and both sides dug in for a static war of attrition.

The USA sought to bring its allies into the war, which became a proxy for the superpower conflict between the USA and the Soviet Union, adopting what became known as the Truman Doctrine. Concerned about its border to the USSR, Turkey sought to become a US ally. It had already signed cooperation agreements and received US military aid. While NATO membership had not yet been approved, Turkey was invited to join other international organisations within the American sphere of influence. Therefore, Ankara agreed to join the 21 nations responding to the UN's call for troops. The injection of US military aid and training also brought about a culture change in the Turkish Armed Forces, which the old guard had resisted during the Second World War, 'A silent struggle took place between these conservatives and the young Turkish officers – the latter winning.'[2]

The first Turkish contingent arrived on 19 October 1950 and in varying strengths, remained until the summer of 1954. The First Turkish Brigade, 5,455 strong, was commanded by Brigadier-General Tahsin Yazic. He was a veteran of Gallipoli in the First

World War and commanded the first Turkish tank battalion in 1937. The Brigade was drawn mainly from the 28th Division and consisted of three infantry battalions from the 241st Infantry regiment, the 2nd Armoured Brigade Artillery Battalion, Light AA Battalion and support units. Troops were taken from the 23rd, 39th and 65th Divisions to bring units up to strength.[3] They advanced into North Korea with the 25th US Division. The Turkish Brigade was attacked by superior enemy forces in Wawon, Kaechon, Kunu-ri and the Sunchon Pass regions. They fought for three days and were encircled several times, each time breaking out successfully. These were the first significant actions the Turkish Army had fought since 1923 and the cost in terms of men and materials was very high. Captain Ismail Catalogy, an aide to General Yazic, explained how they felt;

> Many men are bitter – bitter because of requested air strikes that did not come, a lack of transportation to get us out of our rough spot, a shortage of food and ammunition, and the fact that we were not advised on occasions of withdrawal plans. Some think they were let down by the Americans. But we are explaining that everyone had a bad time up there.[4]

What was left of the Turkish Brigade was moved south to recover and re-organise. They then participated in Operation Thunderbolt in January 1951, while attached to the US Army's IX Corps. This led to another fierce battle around Hill 151. Eventually, the brigade found itself defending against the Chinese spring offensive and forced to retreat south of Seoul, which it completed in admirable fashion. The Republic of Korea awarded the Turks the Presidential Unit Citation for their part in this campaign. However, these offensives were not decisive, and the war developed into a war of patrols supported by artillery and airstrikes.

The Second Turkish Brigade (Brigadier-General Namik Argue) arrived to replace the First in July 1951. In turn, it was relieved by the Third Brigade in July 1952 and then by the Fourth Brigade in September 1953. The replacement brigades saw less action and fewer casualties as the war had moved to the military stalemate phase. Even so, the Turks fought right up to the end of the conflict, with 150 killed in the actions around Elko, Vegas and Carson in May 1953.

In total, 14,936 Turkish troops served in Korea, suffering 3,506 casualties (23 percent of troops committed), including 741 killed. They were generally considered the best of the smaller UN contingents, particularly in defence and close combat when they drew long knives. Max Hastings explained: 'Among the most prominent contributors, the Turks sent a much-respected infantry brigade, whose men were evidently uninterested in higher tactics or sophisticated military skills, but possessed much rugged courage and willingness to endure.'[5]

Turkish troops also exhibited greater discipline and cohesiveness in captivity than other UN units and resisted indoctrination efforts. Of the 229 Turkish prisoners, all survived their captivity.

There were a few challenges in integrating Turkish troops within the US structure, including having pork in US rations; American coffee was not well received, either. Most Turkish soldiers came from poor rural villages in eastern Turkey and only a few officers spoke English. Hardly any American officers spoke Turkish; even the training films had to be translated live. Replacements from Turkey were also slow to arrive and were not proficient in handling the US weapons the brigade had been supplied with. They had few trucks and relied on US transport. The Turkish troops arrived wearing their recently adopted battledress, British Mk 2 steel helmets, and German-pattern ammunition pouches. After the early battles, their

uniforms, helmets and equipment were entirely American, with their own brigade device (red spearhead with white stars) on the right side of the helmet and a national badge (red circle with a white star and crescent) on the top of the right sleeve. Turkish troops were not impressed with the time it took to lace up American issue boots but were grateful to get rid of their British helmets. They described them as a 'soup plate, the most impractical headgear designed by man.' One soldier explained why: 'I tossed my grenade and suddenly everything went black. I couldn't see a thing. My helmet was resting on my nose.'[6]

The Turkish military learned many valuable lessons from their combat experience in Korea, not least ensuring officers could speak English (not that the US or other allies reciprocated in learning Turkish). Turkey also gained economically, militarily and diplomatically from the Turkish contribution to the war, which led to it being accepted into membership of NATO in 1952.

General W. Walker (US Army, and commander of UN Forces in Korea), pinning a Silver Star to Brigadier-General Tahsin Yzici, during the Korea War. (US Army)

Turkey and NATO

Turkey joined NATO in 1952 after two previous applications were denied due to several members feeling the pact would be more effective without vulnerable members in the eastern Mediterranean. The NATO Working Party agreed that while Turkey and Greece could not participate in NATO, steps should be taken to assure them that their security had not been lost sight of. Britain wanted to go further with an explicit Article in the Treaty, but this was rejected by others.[7]

Despite this refusal, Turkey received military aid under the Truman Doctrine, first introduced as a US intervention in the Greek Civil War after the British appealed for US assistance. Truman believed that if Greece fell to the communists, Turkey would be isolated and lost to the Western alliance. In an address to Congress requesting $400 million in aid to Greece and Turkey, he said: 'It must be the policy of the United States to support free peoples who are resisting attempted subjugation by armed minorities or outside pressures.'[8]

US officials told Truman that what diplomacy could not accomplish, firmness could and only by making the Soviets aware that they were prepared 'to meet aggression with force of arms', would prevent Moscow from pressing their demands on Turkey. However, this support was initially limited. For example, requests for funding the modernisation of the Turkish fleet in 1947 were deferred as the funds were unavailable and naval officers doubted whether such aid would deter the Soviets.

The subsequent Military Assistance Programme (MAP) increased support for Turkey to US$100 million in March 1949. Turkey was seen as a source of cheap troops as in 1964, the cost of one American soldier was $6,500 per annum, while one Turkish soldier cost only $235. The TSK did apply some reforms in return for MAP aid; the army was slimmed down from 700,000 to 400,000, the command structure streamlined, and promotion was based more on ability. However, these reforms did not go far enough for many middle-ranking officers, whose contact with Western armies highlighted the scope for initiative rather than the hierarchal traditions of their own military.[9]

Turkey and CENTO

Turkey opposed communist regimes in the Middle East and in February 1955, signed the Baghdad Pact. Also known as the Middle East Treaty Organisation (METO) and since 1958, the Central Treaty Organisation (CENTO), this was a military alliance that joined Iran, Iraq, Pakistan, Turkey and the United Kingdom. The USA was not a member but did join the military committee and began providing military aid to all the members. Modelled on NATO, METO committed the signatory nations to mutual cooperation and protection and non-intervention in each other's affairs. Its goal was to contain the Soviet Union by having a line of strong states along the Soviet Union's south-western frontier. Moreover, two-thirds of the world's known oil reserves of this period were in the Middle East. A US National Security Council report said: 'Turkey's alignment with the free world furnishes a protective screen behind which the defensive strength of the countries in the Eastern Mediterranean can be developed.'[10]

This also reflected the British view of Turkey as a Middle East power; ironically, Turkey saw itself as a European power and was reluctant to be drawn into Middle East conflicts even when CENTO's headquarters moved to Ankara in 1958 (although this pact never had a unified military command structure or US bases). Iraq withdrew the same year, after the British-installed monarchy was overthrown in a coup.[11] Nevertheless, CENTO survived and its funding included a remarkably scenic stretch of railway from Lake Van in Turkey to Sharafkhaneh in Iran and scientific and cultural investment.

At the beginning of the period covered in this book, Turkish military thinking was strongly linked to NATO strategies. However, it started to view NATO as a remote organisation they hoped would be there when required, however, military thinking was along national lines. Most of the air force and navy were allocated to NATO tasks along with part of the land forces; although the Turkish General Staff could re-deploy forces assigned to NATO at their own discretion. The requirement was to notify and explain but it did not require prior approval and this approach percolated down to the rank and file. A Turkish journalist asked a unit of 300 men what NATO was and only five knew the answer; some thought it was a sports club.[12] Officers seconded to NATO generally had a favourable view of their experience. They argued it brought experience they would not otherwise get and helped modernise the TSK.

Guardians of Kemalism

During the 1950s and 1960s, the TSK held a unique place in Turkish society, quite different from that in other Western nations. Its special status was enshrined in legislation and reinforced through the military oath and indoctrination of the armed forces: 'The role of the military in Turkey is rooted in Turkish society, history and culture. The military has always lain at the heart of how Turks define themselves; and most still regard the institution of the military as the embodiment of the highest virtues of the nation.'[13]

While maintaining that it was above politics, the command of the TSK perceived itself as the guardian of the principles (Kemalism) of the republic's founder, Kemal Atatürk. Arguably, the Turkish military had never been linked to just one political party and had never sought permanent power but when its generals believed civilian governments were straying from those principles, they were determined to intervene; mostly formally, but in extremis, through a military coup. This happened in 1960 and again in 1971. However, each time they returned power to civilian governments. This makes Turkey significantly different to so many other military dictatorships – especially in Europe, in the Middle East and Latin America.

Nevertheless, each intervention included longer-term changes that strengthened the position of the armed forces and even outside these periods, the TSK directly intervened through an informal mechanism. It has been argued that for most of the Republican Period, the armed forces effectively shared power with civilian governments. Ironically, while military officers were suffering in the late 1950s – as their modest salaries failed to keep up with high inflation (running at around 16 percent) – and there was a perception that defence budgets were being cut, actually, the government of Prime Minister Adnan Menderes maintained the defence budget at significant cost to economic growth.

General Staff and the Land Forces of the 1960s[14]

Despite the US influence, the General Staff – established along Prussian patterns in the nineteenth century – remained the top staff organisation of the TSK through the 1950s and 1960s (and indeed, until today). Its official purpose was to convert political decisions related to the national security into doctrine, strategy and tactics and thus equip, organise and train personnel for combat and intelligence operations, and provide them with necessary logistic services. As such, it was also the sole military procurement body. Since 1952, the General Staff was also working as a coordination point in the military relations between Turkey and other NATO members. The Chief of the General Staff was usually drafted from the position of the Commander of the Turkish Land Forces and held the fifth-highest rank in the state protocol list, right after the President of the Republic, the President of the Constitutional Court, the Chairman of the Grand National Assembly and the Vice President. While the president was the official Commander-in-Chief of the TSK, controlling the armed forces via the Minister of Defence, at times of war, it was the Chief of the General Staff who acted as the Commander-in-Chief of the Armed Forces in the name of the president.

Finally, the General Staff also exercised direct control over the National Security Service and the Special and Auxiliary Combat Troops. This was established in 1926 and played a key role in the many intelligence operations that took place in Turkey during the Second World War, before being replaced by the National Intelligence Organisation, in 1965. Its purpose was gathering intelligence about the current and potential threats from inside and outside the country and it operated both in Turkey and abroad, with its director reporting to the Office of the Prime Minister (although this did not include warning civilian leaders about military interventions in politics). The latter was a follow-up to the previously-mentioned Special Organisation; established in 1952, it was tasked with carrying out operations that exceeded the capability of other available units.

The various Headquarters of the TSK were situated in Ankara. The General Staff Headquarters was the 'brains' of the 452,000-strong

TURKISH MILITARY COUP D'ETATS

The first successful coup d'etat in the Republic of Turkey took place on 27 May 1990, and was – formally, and at a later stage – led by General Cemal Gürsel. It removed the DP government of Prime Minister Adnan Menderes, which had defeated Atatürk's RPP during elections of 1950. The background of the coup was the end of the US aid under the Marshall Plan, which prompted the government to consider alternative credit from the USSR. Principal coup plotters – actually led by Colonel Alparslan Türkes and including 38 young officers that acted outside the military chain of command – were fiercely anti-communist, although their public explanation for the coup was vague at best. Certainly enough, without the break-down of parliamentary democracy system of rule, it was unlikely that senior military commanders would have ever endorsed it.

The coup led to a purge of generals, officers, judges and university staff. President Celal Bayar, prime minister Adnan Menderes and several administration members, were tried in a court appointed by the junta on the island of Yassiada. The politicians were charged with high treason, misuse of public funds and abrogation of the constitution. The tribunals ended with the execution of Adnan Menderes, the Minister of Foreign Affairs and the Minister of Finance, on 17 September 1961. Celal Bayar was imprisoned for life. Colonel Türkes probably favoured continued military dictatorship, but this was resisted by the majority of top officers, who wanted to return to civilian rule.

A new constitution was approved in a referendum of 9 July 1961 and – after elections of October of the same year – power returned to a new civilian government, However, the military remained dominant in Turkish politics and General Cemal Gürsel was appointed the president; it was Gürsel who began a further modernisation of the Turkish Armed Forces and ordered the intervention on Cyprus of 1964. The legacy of the coup of 1960 was the creation of the Inner Service Act of the TSK, which legitimised the military intervention in politics. From that point onwards, its top brass would make a repeated use to legitimise its similar actions.

Army Colonel Aydemir organised two failed coups, one in February 1962 and another in May 1963. However, he was arrested and executed, demonstrating that the General Staff was

General Cemal Gürsel. Belonging to the last generation of Ottoman-trained officers, he was a veteran of the Gallipoli Campaign. In September 1918, he was captured by the British on the Gaza front and held captive for two years. Upon his return to Turkey, he completed his military education and served with distinction until being appointed the Chief-of-Staff TSK, in 1958. Although authoring the famous letter that both demanded President Bayar to resign and the armed forces to stay out of politics, he subsequently served two terms as the President of the Turkish Republic. (Albert Grandolini Collection)

ready to take action against any unauthorised coup attempts and their wish to maintain the unity of the command structure.

TSK, the second-largest armed forces in NATO. At 5.3 percent of the male population, only Greece (5.8 percent) had a higher proportion of males between 15 and 64 in the armed forces in Europe. The Chief of the General Staff in 1963 was General Cevdet Sunay (in 1966, he became the President of Turkey). He was replaced by General Cemal Tural, who was briefly the President of the Nation Party. Both appointments highlight the close links between the military and politics.

Unlike their NATO counterparts, for most of this period they reported directly to the prime minister rather than the Minister of Defence. They also controlled the budget, which could reach as high as 25 percent of the national budget ($235m in 1962 or 5 percent of GDP). The National Security Council (Milli Güvenlik Kurulu, MGK) was formed in 1962 following the 1960 military coup and was the principal government agency coordinating and developing national security policy. This structure institutionalised the influence of the Turkish military over politics. Policy was expressed

in the National Security Policy Document (Milli Güvenlik Siyaseti Belgesi), commonly known as 'The Red Book'. Another significant difference from Western practice was that the TSK conducted its threat assessment based on the military-led National Intelligence Organisation and their own sources. Civilian ministries' including defence and foreign affairs, played only a limited role.

For equipment, the TSK was almost totally reliant on American surplus stocks. The US had large amounts of surplus weapons after the Second World War and Korea, which were sent to Allies like Turkey and Greece. US General Haig once described this as 'the junkyard', and even these were running out by the 1960s. Turkey had no armaments policy of its own until the late 1960s. By then, defence systems had become much more expensive and the US started donating money rather than equipment; the message being that arms in the future would be available only at a price. In 1972, the donations were replaced by loans due to the rise in Turkish per capita income.

Germany also provided modest military aid from 1964 in the form of grants. As one NATO official put it, 'We can no longer provide everything for the Turkish Armed services as in the 1950s. You have to contribute as well. All we can do is relieve you of some of the financial burden.' Despite this policy, NATO planners were concerned about the absence of modern equipment. In particular, the lack of protection against nuclear, biological and chemical (NBC) weapons, limited air defence and poor command control and communications.

In June 1947, the Pentagon sent a military mission to Turkey, led by General Oliver. He reported it would cost $1.8 billion to convert the TSK into a modern fighting force. This was at a time when just $100m had been allocated under the Truman Doctrine. The mission started in the spring of 1948 and grew to 459 personnel within three years. However, the aid initially provided by the USA was rather short-term; designed to slow down a Soviet offensive, rather than the long-term programmes Turkey wanted. Many US officers felt that while keeping out of the Second World War may have been the best policy for the country, the military fell behind in experience and the use of technology; they also identified problems with the poor transport network and low literacy levels.

Training had traditionally been undertaken at the unit level, and there was resistance to centralised training until 1954, when three training divisions were established. Literacy was addressed with 16 schools created by 1958. Güvenc and Uyar say this was 'Arguably the most successful aspect of US military assistance to Turkey during the Cold War.' The US mission also pressed for more and better trained NCOs, a reform resisted by officers who felt it threatened their command status and privileges.

By the mid-1960s, the USA had provided Turkey with more than US$ 5 billion in foreign aid. About half of this had been direct military assistance. Whilst the mass of the amount went into a huge expansion of the air force and some into the navy, a significant portion was used to modernise and re-organise the army, essentially all major units of which were assigned to NATO. By the mid-1960s, the TKK had a total strength of around 400,000, with 2,500,000 reservists, and was organised into three armies:

- First Army was based in western Turkey: headquartered in Istanbul, it was covering Eastern Thrace and the Straits, aiming to defend against a Warsaw Pact attack from Bulgaria. It faced large Soviet and Bulgarian forces with help of extensive fortifications along the border, and maintained a degree of cooperation with the Greek armed forces.

- Second Army faced the Middle East, including Iraq and Syria, especially the latter of which was widely perceived as a 'Soviet client'.
- Third Army was deployed along the Trans-Caucasus border to the USSR – the traditional Russian invasion route.

Additionally, there were Interior Zones with training divisions, but the deployment along the Aegean Sea was limited and along the Mediterranean coast west of Adana, next to nonexistent. Three national corps headquarters were established within the NATO structures, including:

- XI Corps in Trabzon
- IV Corps in Ankara
- VI Corps in Adana

Further down the chain of command was a total of one armoured division, one mechanised infantry division, 14 infantry divisions (most divisions had five brigades), four armoured cavalry brigades, four armoured brigades, three mechanised infantry brigades, two parachute battalions, and four battalions (420th, 450th, 490th, and 550th) equipped with MGR-1 Honest John tactical ballistic missiles that could be equipped with nuclear warheads from the US arsenals. The equipment of these units was well-streamlined and very similar to that of the US Army. It included around 1,000 M47 and M48 MBTs, around 500 M113 armoured personnel carriers, over 300 M52T self-propelled howitzers 155mm calibre and around 1,000 towed artillery pieces 105mm, 155mm and 103mm calibre. Following the example of the US Army, the TKK also had its own flying branch, the Turkish Army Aviation, flying a miscellany of around 40 aircraft and 20 helicopters. The responsibility for operations in Cyprus was initially assumed by the 39th Infantry Division in Adana and later on, the Commando Brigade and Airborne Brigade, established in 1970 and 1971, respectively.

Apart from conventional units, the TSK included the Tactical Mobilisation Group (Seferberlik Taktik Kurulu, TMG). Established in 1952 as part of NATO's efforts to create a counter-guerrilla force that would work closely with the CIA, this was initially commanded by Brigadier-General Danis Karabelen – a veteran of the Gallipoli campaign and an expert in paramilitary operations trained in the USA in special warfare. The TMG was disbanded in 1965, but the task of special operations was assumed by the Special Warfare Department (Özel Harp Dairesi, OHD) – an organisation that had already helped establish the Turkish armed groups on Cyprus.

A row of M47 Patton MBTs of the TSK, as seen during the training: over 1,000 of such tanks, and much improved M48s, formed the backbone of the Turkish armoured formations of the time. (Albert Grandolini Collection)

TRAINING OF TURKISH MILITARY OFFICERS

An integral part of officer training in the TSK, the ideology of the force was defined in a three-volume textbook emphasising the lessons learned from Turkish history. This focused on protection of the republic from external and internal threats, on identifying separatist and extremist movements and emphasised secularism. In a rare look inside the TSK, Mehmet Ali Birand quoted the speech given to cadets on the first day of their training at the academy:

'Your flag will be the great Atatürk. Your ideology will be his principles, your aim will be the direction he showed us. You will follow unswervingly in Atatürk's footsteps.'

And, if that wasn't enough responsibility, he continued,

'Atatürk put this country in our safekeeping. If you become a soldier and officer worthy of him we will entrust the flag, which means the fatherland, to you. This country will belong to you.'

As of the 1950s and 1960s, military cadets were recruited primarily from rural areas of central Anatolia for the army and the Aegean/Marmara Seas region for the air force and navy. Familial recruitment was common, with cadets largely coming from military or civil service families. The experience of young officers once they joined a unit was pretty demanding. They typically served for 10 years in the field before promotion to captain. While the pay was comparable with civil servants, fringe benefits included housing, health care, shops, holidays and social clubs. The cream of officers entered the staff academies to become staff officers. It was less intensive than other NATO armies (one year instead of two) and more directive and theoretical. Students were also likely to be younger and more junior than their NATO counterparts. Graduates were credited with an extra three years of seniority, received higher pay and were much more likely to get promoted and reach senior ranks. A unique feature was that all three services were trained on the same campus, a self-sufficient small town outside Istanbul, with some 3,000 inhabitants covering over 1,180,000 square metres.

The presence of the US military mission prompted a radical change in the doctrine of the TSK; until the 1950s, this was still based on the Prussian system and granted a high degree of command autonomy to commanders. Convinced there was no TSK unit capable of operating effectively – which, obviously, was a rather harsh conclusion considering the performance of the Turkish Brigade in Korea – in the 1950s, the Americans influenced the retirement of some 80 generals and impressed their detailed field manuals upon the Turks, causing something of a culture shock. Notably, younger officers welcomed the cultural change that US military assistance brought; indeed, it was the events of 1964 that forced Ankara into realising the risks of over-reliance on the USA. Güvenc and Uyar concluded: 'Hence, they had reasons both to appreciate and resent the US military.' 'Such mixed feelings inevitably limited the impact of US assistance on the Turkish military during the Cold War.'

Turkish Navy

Established in the early fourteenth century, when the Ottomans captured Karamürsel with a naval shipyard, the Ottoman Navy initially experienced centuries of near-constant growth, while establishing itself as the dominant power in the Mediterranean also capable of running raids well into northern Europe. However, during the seventeenth century, it experienced a period of stagnation from which it never fully recovered. Arguably, in the eighteenth century, it suffered as many defeats as it achieved victories but then began lagging in regards to its technological development. Nowhere did this become as obvious as during successive wars with Russia. It was only after the Battle of Navarino in 1827, that Sultan Mahmud II gave priority to the construction of a new fleet equipped with steam-powered vessels. The result being several of the largest warships of the line ever built. By 1875, the Ottoman Navy had 21 of these, 173 other warships and was ranked the third largest in the world.

However, another disastrous war, the related financial burden and the lack of heavy industry necessary to support modernisation, sealed the fate of the service. A recovery attempt initiated after the coup of 1908 proved too little too late; both the Italo-Turkish War of 1911–1912 and the Balkan War of 1912–1913, were disastrous for the Ottoman Navy. Another attempt at re-building was initiated in 1913–1914, but the two dreadnoughts ordered (and paid for) from Great Britain, were confiscated by London due to the outbreak of the First World War.

Indeed, this act contributed to the Ottoman decision to side with Central Powers – which was partially compensated when the German battlecruiser SMS *Goeben* and light cruiser SMS *Breslau* arrived at the Dardanelles and entered service with the Ottoman Navy as *Yavuz Sultan Selim* and *Midili*, respectively. The two modern vessels significantly bolstered a fleet of a mere seven other major vessels, including two old battleships – *Turgut Reis* (ex-SMS *Weissenburg*) and *Barbaros Hayreddin* (ex-SMS *Kurfürst Friedrich Wilhelm*) – acquired earlier from Germany.

The navy thus began the First World War by raiding Russian ports in the Black Sea but was then forced to withdraw from the Mediterranean and its actions during the Gallipoli campaign were limited to minelayers deploying mines in the Dardanelles Strait. The British submarine HMS *E11* – which raided the Marmara Sea for months, sinking 27 steamers and 58 smaller vessels in the process – sank the battleship *Barbaros Hayreddin* on 8 August 1915. The last large action of the Ottoman Navy took place on 20 January 1918, when *Yavuz Sultan Selim* and *Midili* managed to sink the British warships HMS *Raglan* and HMS *M28* and a transport ship off Mudros, in Greece. However, on the way back, *Midili* ran into a minefield between Lemnos and Gökceada, hit five mines and sank. After the end of the First World War, the Ottoman Navy was dissolved and its large ships impounded in the Sea of Marmara.

Reconstructed on the establishment of the Turkish Republic, the navy experienced beneficial growth through the late 1920s and during the 1930s. However, despite a well-developed shipyard and arsenal at the Gulf of Izmir, it continued purchasing smaller warships from Great Britain, Italy and submarines from Germany. By 1949, it still had one battlecruiser, three destroyers, a few submarines and a miscellany of minelayers and minehunters in operations, when a new effort to modernise and expand was initiated – this time with US support. The flagship, battlecruiser *Yavuz*, was decommissioned in 1950 (and sold for scrapping in 1971), as was a miscellany of warships of British and Italian design, most of which were retired by 1954–1955. Instead, the destroyer-fleet was renewed by a total of

In the course of modernisation of the 1930s, the Turkish Navy acquired four Project 280/Ay-class submarines based on the German Type IX-ocean-going vessels. Two were constructed in Germany (including *Saldiray*, visible here), while two – *Atlay* and *Yildray* – were completed at the Taskizak Shipyard in Istanbul. (Albert Grandolini Collection)

Below: Battlecruiser *Yavuz* in Istanbul of 1947, only three years before retirement. (USN photo)

four *Gleaves*-class vessels from the USA, followed by four *M*-class destroyers acquired from Great Britain in 1959. While US ships were largely left in their original condition, those of British origin had their aft set of torpedo tubes and some of secondary armament removed, received a new deckhouse and Squid anti-submarine weapons system.

Even more emphasis was put on the expansion of the submarine fleet; older vessels of British, Italian and German designs were all decommissioned between 1947 and 1949, and replaced by 11 boats of the *Balao*-class, acquired in two batches, one in 1948–1954 and the other between 1958 and 1960, The mine-warfare component was expanded to more than 20 vessels, primarily of Canadian and US design, acquired through the mid-1940s, but the amphibious assault fleet was limited to four British constructed vessels of the AG 4-class.

As of 1963, the commander of the Turkish Navy was Admiral Necdet Uran. Headquartered in Ankara, his forces were organised into two commands (Northern Area and Southern Area), had their main base at Gölcük, in the Sea of Marmara and boasted the strength of 1,400 officers and 31,000 other ranks. Naval policy had been focused on coastal defence since the early years of the Turkish Republic; this strategy remained valid once Turkey came under the NATO security umbrella and only started to shift in the twenty-first century.

Table 3: Major Warships of the Turkish Navy, 1963–1967

Hull Number	Name	Type	Origin
D-344	Gaziantep	gun destroyer	ex-*Lansdowne* (DD-486; USA)
D-346	Giresun	"	ex-*McCalla* (DD-488; USA)
D-346	Gelibolu	"	ex-*Buchanan* (DD-484; USA)
D-347	Gemlik	"	ex-*Lardner* (DD-487; USA)
D-348	Alp Alslan	"	ex-*Milne* (G14; UK)
D-349	Maresal Fevzi Cakmak	"	ex-*Mame* (G35; UK)
D-350	Kilic Ali Pasa	"	ex-*Matchless* (G52; UK)
D-351	Piyale Pasa	"	ex-*Meteor* (G73; UK)
S-330	Birinci İnönü	attack submarine	ex-*Brill* (SS-330; USA)
S-331	Ikinci İnönü	"	ex-*Blueback* (SS-326; USA)
S-332	Sakarya	"	ex-*Boarfish* (SS-327; USA)
S-333	Canakkale	"	ex-*Bumper* (SS-333; USA)
S-334	Gür	"	ex-*Chub* (SS-329; USA)
S-335	Dumlupinar	"	ex-*Blower* (SS-325; USA)
S-340	Preveze	"	ex-*Guitarro* (SS-363; USA)
S-341	Cerbe	"	ex-*Hammerhead* (SS-364; USA)
S-342	Turgutreis	"	ex-*Bergall* (SS-320; USA)
S-343	Piri Reis	"	ex-*Mapiro* (SS-376; USA)
S-344	Hizirreis	"	ex-*Mero* (SS-378; USA)

The *Balao*-class submarine *Piri Reis* (S-343), as seen after its transfer to the Turkish Navy. The *Balaos* were largest class of submarines ever constructed for the US Navy; a total of 120 were commissioned during the Second World War. They were similar to the *Gato*-class but had a better maximum diving depth (140m/450ft). Three of the boats supplied to Turkey were modified within the GUPPY programme, receiving a streamlined sail with the fleet snorkel. (USN photo)

ALP ARSLAN-CLASS

The British-made M or Milne-Class destroyers were regarded as one of the most successful of the Royal Navy in the 1940s and 1950s; they were the first British vessels of this type to have power-worked main gun turrets. The ships were designed to reach a maximum speed of 36 knots and had a range of 10,200km. HMS *Milne* was completed in 1942 and saw service in the Mediterranean and Arctic theatres of operations. HMS *Matchless* escorted Winston Churchill to the USA in 1943 and helped finish the German battlecruiser *Scharnhorst* with

torpedoes. Four ships of the class were transferred to Turkey in 1959, following a refit in British yards: in Turkish service they were named *Alp Arslan*, *Kilicali Pasha*, *Piyale Pasha*, and *Maresal Fevzi Cakmak*. Their main armament of six 4.7in (114mm) guns, with six Bofors 40mm and two 3-pdr guns was retained, but one of torpedo-launchers was removed and instead, a triple-barrelled Squid depth charge mortar was installed. In Turkish service, all were named after famous admirals and generals.

A Milne-Class destroyer HMS *Meteor*, as seen in around 1947, about a dozen years before being overhauled and transferred to the Turkish Navy. Clearly visible is the main armament consisting of three turrets, each with twin 4.7in/114mm guns. (Albert Grandolini Collection)

Turkish Air Force of the 1950s and 1960s[15]

The Ottomans experienced immense problems while trying to establish a flying branch of their armed forces. As it was, the first group of officers were sent to France for aviator training in 1911 and a year later, Deperdussin, Bleriot, Rep, Prier-Dickson and Harlan aircraft were acquired and operated from the Yesilköy military airfield west of Istanbul.

However, as of 1913, the activity of the Ottoman fliers was limited to observation flights over the front and – sporadically – dropping bombs over the Bulgarian trenches. Immediately after the Balkan Wars, the Ottoman Army Aviation Service was reorganised with French support and by 1914, large orders for aircraft were placed in Paris and London. However, all the French personnel left in August of that year and only one aeroplane was delivered. Thus, the Ottoman Army Aviation Service entered the First World War with only six operational aircraft and six pilots and it was up to Germany to supply both modern equipment and the personnel necessary to expand the force.

By 1917, the service expanded through the acquisition of more than 200 aircraft, organised into 15 'companies' (most of these comparable to 'flights'). However, there were extensive maintenance problems and combat losses were heavy and at the time of the Moudros armistice, the Ottoman aviation was down to just 25 operational aircraft, without German logistics support, and with its 35 pilots and 44 observers scattered along the disintegrating fronts. While the Entente forces are known to have seized 45 aircraft in the Istanbul area, the nationalists managed to hide another 17 – most of them in derelict condition – in the east; however, under the terms of the Treaty of Versailles, the country was prohibited from owning and operating military aircraft. Nevertheless, in 1920, a new 'Air Force Branch' was established by nationalist forces commanded by Atatürk. By 1922, this was expanded through more than 30 aircraft being handed over by the French in Syria or procured from Italy and it saw intensive operations during the final campaign against the Greek Army in western Anatolia.

Being 'air minded', Atatürk sought to promote and finance the growth of aviation. The Turkish Air League was already founded in 1923; a School for Aviation Mechanics established in Yesilköy in 1926, while pilots were largely trained in France. In 1927, the League was reorganised as the Turkish Air Force (*Hava Kuvvetleri Komutanligi*, HVKK) and – after abandoning the idea of launching production of

Rohrbach fighters of Danish origin due to fierce French competition – began acquiring modern fighters from France and the USA.

Through the 1930s, the service continued growing principally under French tuition: it was greatly expanded and reorganised and by 1938, some 450 qualified pilots were flying more than 300 aircraft. During that year, RAF instructors were seconded to the HVKK and the force was remodelled along British ideas. London continued selling combat aircraft to Istanbul despite its acquisition of German combat aircraft and a non-aggression pact with Berlin, in 1941. In fact, when Turks experienced problems maintaining their Heinkel He.111 bombers, the British began supplying spares salvaged from aircraft of this type shot down over Great Britain.

The Western powers continued increasing their support through 1942, 1943 and 1944, even after Istanbul purchased 72 Focke Wulf Fw.190A fighters from Berlin. As a consequence, by 1945, the HVKK was further expanded and flew a highly unusual miscellany of – between others – Bristol Beaufighters, Bristol Beaufots, Bristol Blenheims, Consolidated B-24D Liberators, de Havilland Mosquito, Fw,190s, Hawker Hurricanes, Martin Baltimores, Supermarine Spitfires – organised into two divisions and 10 regiments. In 1947, the US Congress approved the supply of the first of large tranches of military aid and an Air Mission was deployed in Turkey. US engineers modernised most of the available air bases, while Republic P-47D Thunderbolt fighter-bombers, North American T-6 Texan and Beech T-11B Kansan trainers, Douglas B-26C Invader light bombers and Douglas C-47 Dakota transports, were supplied from surplus stocks of the US Army Air Force.

As soon as Turkey became a member of NATO, in 1952 the pace of systematic re-organisation and modernisation picked up. Existing air bases were rebuilt and expanded again, new airfields, arms and fuel depots, oil pipelines, communication facilities and a network of seven major early warning radar stations were constructed. The US Air Force established a big training mission at Eskisehir, where hundreds of pilots and ground personnel underwent training on T-6s and T-11s, while an Operational Training Unit came into being at Diyarbakir. Hundreds of jets followed. The first two T-33As arrived in December 1951 and over the following month, enough were delivered to form a jet training squadron at Balikesir.

In January 1952, the first out of 90 F-84Gs delivered that year were in service. No less than 135 followed in 1953 and another 83 in 1954, while the number of T-33As was increased to 48 by 1955. Between

Turkey received well over 250 Republic F-84G Thunderjets during the first half of the 1950s. They remained in service with at least two units of the TSK as of 1963–1964. Notable on this example are the band around the intake, fin strip and arrows on the wing-trip drop tank, all used as identification of its assignment to a specific base. (Albert Grandolini Collection)

1954 and 1956, the HVKK also received 107 refurbished Canadair Sabre F.Mk 2s and F.Mk 4s to establish two interceptor wings with three squadrons each, while in 1955 it was handed a total of 46 RF-84F Thunderflashes for two reconnaissance squadrons. Atop of this, between 1955 and 1958, Ankara received another 172 F-84Gs from surplus NATO-stocks, to replace peace-time attrition and create some reserve; in total, the HVKK thus received no less than 480 Thunderjets, of which about 235 were still in service as of 1960.

Meanwhile, shortly after the Makina ve Kimya Endustrisi Kurumu enterprise launched the production of the indigenous M.K.E.K.4 Ugur primary trainer, the training system was completely reformed. Instead of being run in the USA and Canada, it was re-located back to Turkey, where the Air Training Command came into being in 1956. This included the Flight School at Gaziemir AB and the Air War School at Güzelyali. In total, the two facilities had four flying squadrons, of which one was equipped with T-6s, another with Ugurs, the third with T-6Cs and Beechcraft T-34A Mentors, while the fourth flew AT-11s and C-47s.

Eventually, once reformed, almost the entire tactical component of the HVKK – the 1st and 3rd Tactical Air Forces, comprising a total of three interceptors, 12 fighter-bombers and one reconnaissance squadron listed in the Table 4 – was assigned to the 6th Allied Tactical Air Force (ATAF) of NATO. Headquartered at Izmir, this also included most of the RHAF.

This intensive period of the HVKK's build-up was still not over when a new one was initiated. In 1958, the HVKK began receiving North American F-100D/F Super Sabres; a total of 48 of these arrived by the end of 1959, replacing F-84Gs of 111 and 113 Filo. Moreover, in 1959–1960, 65 F-84Fs of the French Air Force were acquired to re-equip the 181 and 183 Filo at Diyarbakir, while another 19 delivered in 1961, entered service with 192 Filo, further reinforced by 35 ex-French RF-84Fs in 1963–1964. By that time, units of the 4th Air Base had already converted to Lockheed F-104G Starfighters supplied via the Mutual Assistance Programme, the first 34 of which were delivered in May 1963. Reinforced by 12 additional examples (including two RF-104Gs) by 1965, the Starfighters initially equipped two squadrons plus an operational conversion unit and had the nuclear strike role as their primary task (as usual at the time and ever since, the nuclear bombs in question came from the US arsenal and required an approval from Washington for their deployment).

Meanwhile, as Germany and the Netherlands withdrew their F-84Fs from service, a total of 185 of these were refurbished and upgraded to the F-84Q standard and delivered to Turkey by 1966. During the same year, personnel of the 161 Squadron (Filo), began converting to the first out of 75 – eventually increased to 140 – F-5A/B Freedom Fighters ordered by Ankara. This unit received air

Table 4: Major Units of the Turkish Air Force, 1958

Wing	Squadron	Base	Aircraft Type & Notes
Air Defence Command (former 2nd Tactical Air Force), HQ Ankara			
ADC Fighter Station		Merzifon	ground control system networking 7 ground-based early warning radar stations
15th Missile Base		Istanbul	Nike Ajax SAM
1st Tactical Air Force, HQ Ankara			
1st Air Base	111 Filo	Eskisehir	F-84G (converting to F-100)
	112 Filo	"	F-84G
	113 Filo	"	F-84G (to F-100 in 1959)
	114 Filo	"	RF-84F
6th Air Base	161 Filo	Bandirma	F-84G
	162 Filo	"	F-84G
	163 Filo	"	F-84G
9th Air Base	191 Filo	Balikesir	F-84G
	192 Filo	"	F-84G (to F-84F in 1960)
	193 Filo	Konya	F-84G; weapons training unit
3rd Tactical Air Force, HQ			
4th Air Base	141 Filo	Diyarbakir	Sabre F.Mk 2/4
	142 Filo	Merzifon	Sabre F.Mk 2/4
	143 Filo	"	Sabre F.Mk 2/4
8th Air Base	181 Filo	Diyarbakir	F-84G (to F-84F in 1959–1960)
	182 Filo	"	F-84G
	183 Filo	"	F-84G (to F-84F in 1959–1960)
	184 Filo	"	RF-84F
12th Air Communications Base	221 Filo	Etimesgut	C-47
	222 Filo	"	C-47
	224 Filo	"	C-47
	225 Filo	"	C-47
	Flight	"	H-19
Air Training Command, HQ Gaziemir			
2nd Air Base		Gaziemir	T-6 & Ugur
3rd Air Base		Güzelyali	T-6, T-34, AT-11, C-47

defence as its primary task, with close support as secondary. That said, the US policy of the time was to supply F-5s in a gradual fashion and Northrop received huge orders from many customers. Thus, the conversion of additional HVKK units to this type was to continue for years longer. Meanwhile, the ADC was disbanded in 1962 and its units re-distributed to tactical air forces. These were further reinforced through the construction of several new air bases and the establishment of additional units, resulting in the composition of the HVKK as listed in the Table 5.

Table 5: Major Units of the Turkish Air Force, 1963–1967

Wing	Squadron	Base	Aircraft Type & Notes
1st Tactical Air Force, HQ Ankara (incl. Air Defence District Command)			
1st Air Base	111 Filo	Eskisehir	F-100D/F
	112 Filo	"	F-100D/F
	114 Filo	"	RF-84F
4th Air Base	141 Filo	Mürted	F-104G
	144 Filo	"	F-104G
6th Air Base	161 Filo	Bandirma	F-84G (to F-5A/B in 1966)
	162 Filo	"	F-84G
	163 Filo	"	F-84Q (to F-A/B in 1967)
9th Air Base	191 Filo	Balikesir	F-84F
	193 Filo	"	F-84G (to F-84Q in 1965)
15th Missile Base		Istanbul	Nike Ajax SAM
3rd Tactical Air Force, HQ Diyarbakir (incl. Air Defence District Command)			
5th Air Base	142 Filo	Merzifon	Sabre F.Mk 2/4 (to F-5A/B in 1967)
	143 Filo	"	Sabre F.Mk 2/4
7th Air Base	113 Filo	Erhac	F-100D/F
	182 Filo	"	RF-84F
8th Air Base	181 Filo	Diyarbakir	F-84F (to F-84Q in 1966)
	183 Filo	"	F-84G (to F-84Q in 1966)
	184 Filo	"	RF-84F
12th Air Communications Base	221 Filo	Etimesgut	C-47
	222 Filo	"	C-47
	223 Filo	"	C-47
	224 Filo	"	C-47
	225 Filo	"	C-47
	Flight	"	H-19
Air Training Command, HQ Gaziemir			
2nd Jet Training Air Base	121 Filo	Izmir	T-33A
	122 Filo	"	T-37A
3rd Jet Training Air Base	131 Filo	Konya	T-37C
	132 Filo	"	T-37C
	192 Filo	"	F-84F, RF-84F, T-33A, AT-11A; weapons training unit

SUPERSONIC FATHER

The F-100 Super Sabre was the single most important combat aircraft in service with the HVKK during the Cyprus Crisis of 1963–1974. It was the first supersonic fighter-bomber to enter service with USAF, where it became known under the nickname 'Hun'. Originally designed as an air superiority fighter and acquired in large numbers, due to suffering from different design-related issues early on, it was relegated to the ground support role. In this role, it flew more combat sorties during the Vietnam War than all other types operated by the USAF combined. The HVKK received two main variants – F-100C and F-100D – both of which had four internal auto canons of 20mm calibre which could carry different combinations of external weapons up to 7,040lbs in total. In clean configuration, the type could reach a maximum speed of 924mph (Mach 1.4) and had a range of nearly 2,000 miles. The first F-100s arrived in Turkey on 16 October 1958. They were followed by more than 200 F-100C/D/Fs, mostly from USAF surplus stocks and 21 from the Danish Air Force. The first group of Turkish F-100-pilots were highly experienced veterans with 800 flight hours and three years of operational service. All converted to the type at Eskisehir in Turkey under US instruction. They were regarded as elite pilots and enjoyed special privileges, including dedicated rest lounges. In Turkish service, the type was nicknamed the *Baba* (Father), due to its 'mature' looks, strong construction, and trusted flight characteristics.

The F-100D with the US FY-serial number 54-2219 was one of 33 jets of this variant delivered to Turkey in 1959, when it entered service with the 112 Filo (nickname 'Korsan'). As usual for the early 1960s, it received gaudy insignia in form of a big lightning bolt in yellow and black on the forward fuselage and a chevron in the same colours on the fin. The squadron continued flying the 'Baba' until 1972, when it was re-designated as 171 Filo. (Albert Grandolini Collection)

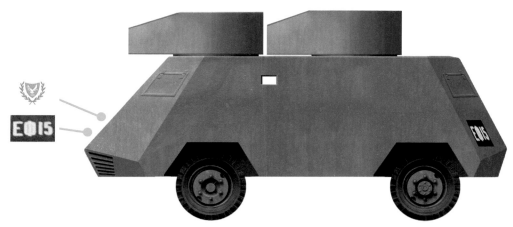

The lack of armour prompted the CNG into constructing improvised armoured vehicles. One of the most numerous improvisations was based on the chassis of the Commer FC, a commercial vehicle designed in Great Britain and manufactured in 1960. Most received a relatively simple, trapezoidal armoured superstructure; additionally, this example operated by the 7th Regular Group of the CNG in Limassol of early 1964, received two turrets for machine guns. Painted in light green overall, it wore the designation EΦ 15 (abbreviation for 'National Guard 15' in Greek language) on the right side of the front and left side of the rear hull, along with the Cypriot coat of arms. (Artwork by David Bocquelet)

Another 'improvised' armoured vehicle of the CNG was this armoured personnel carrier based on the chassis of a Valentine Mk II/Mk III infantry tank, abandoned by a copper mining company and then recovered from a quarry and restored to working order. It lacked the turret and thus received an armoured superstructure, before being shown on a parade in Limassol on 1 April 1964. It was armed with machine guns that fired through the slits and wore the Cypriot coat of arms on the front and the designation EΦ 19 on the front and the rear of the hull. Painted in dark desert sand colour overall, it was deployed in combat by the 7th Regular Group of the CNG in Limassol, February 1964. (Artwork by David Bocquelet)

Marmon-Herrington of South Africa, manufactured thousands of armoured cars based on commercial chassis during the Second World War. About 40 of the Marmon-Herrington Mk IVF cars were inherited by the Greek Cypriots (together with four Shorlands and two Daimler Dingos) and pressed into service by the CNG. Several were knocked out by fire of TMT's recoilless rifles and then by THK air strikes during the attack on the Kokkina area, in August 1964. As far as is known, at the time, all were painted in dark green overall (later replaced by a lighter shade) and wore small white crosses on blue quadrants, applied on the turret sides for identification purposes. (Artwork by David Bocquelet)

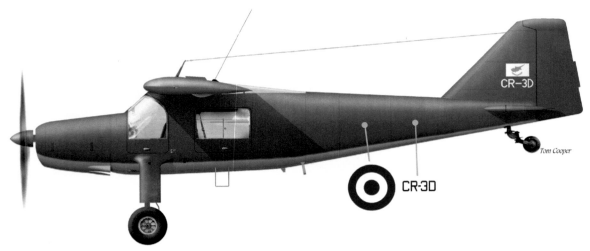

This is a reconstruction of the sole Dornier Do.27A of the 1st Air Squadron/Cyprus Flight, CNG – probably the most frequently-flown aircraft operated by Greek Cypriots during the crisis of 1963–1964, usually piloted by the CO of that unit, Captain Antonios Vogiatzakis. Sadly, there are no photographs of it in Cyprus, but it is known to have been acquired in Germany in 1961, with the registration 5B-CAA. At the time, it appears to have worn the livery shown here, in *Bronzegrün* (RAL 6031) on upper surfaces and sides, and *Hellblau* (RAL 5012) on undersurfaces. It is known to have received the Cypriot flag and registration CR-3D, but it remains unknown how and where they were applied; either in white on the fin (instead of the former German registration) or – together with the Greek roundel – in black on the rear fuselage. This Do.27A survived the crisis but was later replaced by a Do.27Q, wearing the same registration. (Artwork by Tom Cooper)

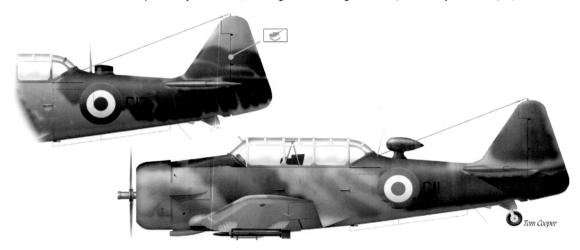

These are reconstructions of two of the North American T-6C/D Texan/Harvards (all upgraded to T-6G-standard) of the RHAF unit destined for deployment to Cyprus. Both are based on takes from the Greek movie *Rendezvous in the Skies*, filmed in 1965 and widely considered as the sole available reference for the appearance of two aircraft: one with the probable serial C11 (main artwork) and C13 (insert). The T-6Gs in question are known to have worn serials in the range C1 to C13 and the RHAF national insignia but should have received the Cypriot flag either on the fin or on the rear fuselage. All were armed with attachment for five 2.75in/70mm unguided rockets under each wing but received no gun pods. Their original bare metal overall livery was crudely over-sprayed with dark sand or tan and dark green, perhaps also some brown; undersides seem to have been left unpainted. (Artwork by Tom Cooper)

Something like the 'unsung heroes' of the RHAF involvement in the Cyprus Crisis of 1963–1964 were the Douglas C-47 Dakota transports of the 355th Mira. This example – serial number 92-622 – is depicted as deployed by a flight of the 13th Squadron sent to support the UN forces in Korea; apparently, the livery of Greek Dakotas changed very little over the following 15 years. Most were left in bare metal overall, but had an 'anti-glare panel' and parts of the forward and rear under fuselage painted in black. The same dark blue used for application of their national insignia was used to apply the number 9 behind the rear cockpit and the band around the forward part of the engine nacelles. Most received full service titles down the upper part of the centre fuselage – all in black. This example also received the nickname 'Neptune'. (Artwork by Luca Canossa)

One of first RHAF units activated in reaction to the Cyprus crisis was the 337th Mira, which was tasked with protection of the southern Aegean and the Dodecanese islands. For this purpose, the squadron regularly rotated pairs or fourships of North American F-86D Sabre Dog interceptors to Souda AB, sometimes also to Kasteli airfield, both on Crete. This is a reconstruction of one of the jets known to have been deployed: F-86D with the US FY-serial number 51-13398, which went into action while still wearing the original unit insignia on the fin (a ghost with two orange bombs, pointing at the squadrons nickname, 'Fantasma'). Standard armament of 337 Mira's Sabre Dogs during the crisis included a pair of GAR-8 infra-red homing air-to-air missiles (AIM-9B Sidewinder) on underwing pylon, and an internal launcher with 24 unguided rockets 2.75in/70mm calibre. (Artwork by Tom Cooper)

Another of the 337th Mira's F-86D Sabre Dogs rotated to the Souda AB in 1964, was this example, wearing the US FY-serial number 51-6217. As usual for the 1950s and most of the 1960s, the jet was left in bare metal overall; had the 'last five' of its serial applied on the fin, and the 'buzz number' prefixed by FU applied on the forward fuselage. For much of the late 1960s, this jet also had most of its rear fuselage and fin painted in red, for exercise purposes, but this colour was removed by 1964. Instead, it received a modified unit insignia in form of 'Fantasma' (ghost) with two orange GAR-8 air-to-air missiles, to denote its principal armament. (Artwork by Tom Cooper)

At the peak of the Cyprus Crisis, in August 1964, the 111th Wing of the RHAF, home-based at Nea Anchialos, is known to have been ordered to prepare F-84F Thunderstreaks of its 338 and 339 Mira for action over the troubled island. The jets in question were all left in bare metal overall, but many wore ID-bands in yellow and blue around their front fuselage and the unit insignia (in this case that of the 338th Mira) behind the rear portion of the cockpit. Typical weapons load included two 460 US gallons drop tanks under inboard underwing hardpoints, a pair of AN/M64A-1 bombs 500lbs/250kg on outboard pylons and four unguided rockets 2.75in/70mm calibre (two under each wing) under the wingtips. To help them lift off, they received a tray with four JATO bottles underneath the rear portion of the centre fuselage. (Artwork by Tom Cooper)

On 17 August 1964, six RF-84F Thunderflashes of the 348th Mira were sent into the (first officially confirmed) reconnaissance operation over Cyprus (an earlier mission, flown in May, remains unconfirmed until today) and thus, became some of very few RHAF aircraft that ever actually operated over the island. This reconstruction is based on information provided by the formation leader, Efthimios Roulias; it is shown the RF-84F with the US FY-serial number 53-8740 as during that sortie. The jet was left in bare metal overall but had an anti-glare panel in dark green along the top of the forward fuselage and the top of its intakes typically painted in dark red and black. According to Roulias, it wore roundels in six positions on 17 August 1964, but no fin flashes; some of 348th Miras actually had all their national insignias removed during the time. (Artwork by Tom Cooper)

Another of six RF-84Fs of the 348th Mira sent to take reconnaissance photographs of Cyprus on 17 August 1964 was this example with the US FY-serial number 53-7588. Its general appearance closely resembled that of the 54-8740 previously illustrated. However, a photograph of this aircraft with all pilots of that squadron, taken in May 1964, shows it not only wearing the full national insignia (except for the fin flash), but also the unit's crest near the top of the fin. Notably, all six RF-84Fs that flew this mission launched with help of four JATO bottles attached near the centre of the bottom fuselage; these were jettisoned once the aircraft were airborne. (Artwork by Tom Cooper)

Originally established in Egypt of 1917, No. 111 (Fighter) Squadron, RAF, was a unit with a rich tradition of operations in the Middle East by the time it deployed 11 of its jets to Cyprus for an annual exercise, in 1964. This is how its English Electric Lightning F.Mk 3 interceptors became involved in monitoring – and then intercepting – Greek and Turkish aerial operations in August 1964; reportedly, none of the jets were armed during such operations. As of the time, all of No. 111 Squadron's jets were left in bare metal overall but also wore the unit's colours (black and yellow) applied from the cockpit down the spine and over all of the fin, with a large squadron crest and the code. This jet's serial number – XR712 – was applied in black on the rear fuselage and repeated on both of the undersurfaces of the wing. (Artwork by Tom Cooper)

Republic RF-84F Thunderflash reconnaissance jets of the THK were some of first Turkish jets to become involved in the Cyprus Crisis. As far as is known, they flew the first few reconnaissance operations over the island – but also over the Aegean Sea and the Dodecanese islands – in December 1963. This example with the US FY-serial number 51-1854, was operated by 184 Akrep (Scorpion) Filo from Diyarbakir from 1964; a unit known to have also been involved in Cyprus operations. Most of the Thunderflashes of the 184 Filo are known to have worn a prominent unit insignia on their fuselage sides, usually applied on a white disc, right behind the camera compartment. (Artwork by Tom Cooper)

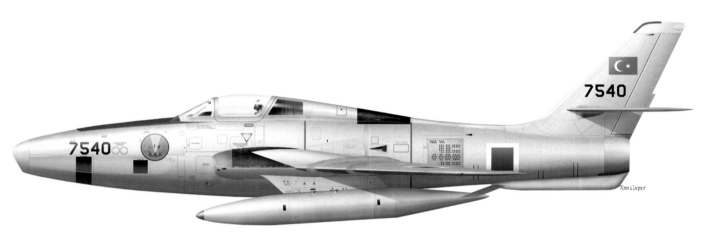

Another THK unit operating RF-84Fs and known to have flown operational sorties over Cyprus in 1964, was the 114 Filo, home-based at Eskisehir AB. As far as is known, all of its jets were left in bare metal overall, wore contemporary national insignia in six positions and fin flashes in standard positions. This example – wearing the US FY-serial number 52-7540 – also received the squadron crest of 114 Filo applied on the rear portion of the camera compartment, on either side of the jet. Notably, tips of drop tanks were painted in red, denoting assignment to the First Jet Base in Eskisehir. The Greeks claimed two RF-84Fs shot down over Cyprus: 52-8871 on 5 June 1964 and another example on 25 November 1967. Neither claim proved true but one of the Turkish Thunderflashes crashed after experiencing mechanical problems on the way back from a sortie over the island. (Artwork by Tom Cooper)

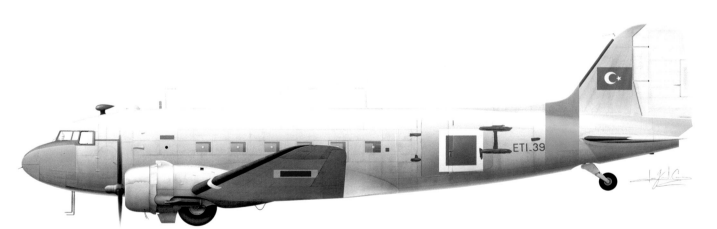

On 8 August 1964, when Ankara decided to actually launch a military intervention on Cyprus and the THK was ordered into action, it took several hours to re-deploy numerous of its fighter-bombers to air bases closer to the island – of which at the time there were next to none in southern Turkey. This re-deployment was supported by Douglas C-47 Dakota transports drawn from all five units operating this type at the time (including 221, 222, 223, 224 and 225 Filos), which hauled ground personnel, ground equipment, spares and weapons to airfields closer to the combat zone. This example wearing the serial ETI_39 is depicted as photographed a few years later, by when the Turkish C-47 fleet was re-deployed from Etimesgut to Gaziemir AB. (Artwork by Luca Canossa)

Initiated in 1958, deliveries of 50 North American F-100D Super Sabres were a matter of pride in Turkey, which in turn, became obvious in their gaudy markings. This example belonged to the first unit declared operational on this type, 111 Filo, from Eskisehir AB. Squadrons home-based there were marking noses of their aircraft in red and white and this jet (US FY-serial 54-2276) also received the 'Panther' insignia of 111 Filo. As usual for the period, the jet was otherwise left in bare metal overall. Originally intended to serve the THK's long-range intercept capabilities and armed with GAR-8 air-to-air missiles and four internal 20mm cannons, during the Cyprus Crisis of 1964, they were deployed as fighter-bombers armed with M117 general purpose bombs and BLU-1B napalm tanks. (Artwork by Tom Cooper)

This is a reconstruction of the F-100D (US FY-serial number 55-2766) flown by Captain Cengiz Töpel when he was shot down off the coast of Cyprus on 8 August 1964. Notably, the light blue and white bands on the nose of this F-100D were indicative of an aircraft home-based at Diyarbakir AB, but this jet was operated by 112 Filo home-based at Eskisehir, the big 'red devil' insignia of which was applied on the forward fuselage. The last three digits of the serial were repeated on the front cover of the front undercarriage, which was also painted in light blue. The unit also applyed chevrons in light blue (outlined in black) on the fins of its jets and the 'devil's fork' in black down the sides of their drop tanks. The jet is illustrated as armed with a combination of M117 general purpose bombs (inboard underwing pylon) and BLU-1B napalm tanks (outboard underwing pylon). (Artwork by Tom Cooper)

Two THK squadrons home-based at Diyarbakir AB as of August 1964 and involved in combat operations over Cyprus, were equipped with ex-French F-84Qs: these were 181 and 183 Filo, the aircraft of which wore the nose band of that base, in light blue and white. As far as is known, except for national insignia (in six positions) and fin flashes, Thunderstreaks of these two squadrons were left in bare metal overall and wore no other insignia. This jet (US FY-serial number 52-8818) is illustrated as armed with BLU-1B napalm tank installed under the outboard underwing pylon. (Artwork by Tom Cooper)

As of August 1964, 192 Filo was a weapons training unit home-based at the 3rd Jet Training Base, at Konya AB and flying a mix of F-84Fs, RF-84Fs, T-33As and AT-11As. Between the jets it operated was this F-84F (US FY-serial number 52-8878), photographed while preparing for a mission over Cyprus. The jet is shown as armed with a single AN/M64A1 bomb (developed during the Second World War but re-equipped with a longer tail for operations from high-speed jets) and four unguided rockets 2.75in/70mm calibre. (Artwork by Tom Cooper)

The THK still had a few units operating obsolete 'straight wing' F-84G Thunderjet fighter-bombers in 1964: except for the 192 Filo, these were 163, 191 and 193 Filo, of which the former two were meanwhile converting to F-84Fs. At least one of these is reported to have flown air strikes on 8 and 9 August 1964. Their precise weapons' configuration remains unclear but probably included the older version of AN/M64A1 bombs with 'short' fins. It is possible that they were also loaded with up to eight 2.75in/70mm unguided rockets (four under each wing). This Thunderjet (US FY-serial number 51-10920) is known to have served with 191 or 193 Filo from Balikesir AB at the time.

While NATO was relatively late with delivering Lockheed F-104G Starfighters to Greece, by 1964, the THK already had two units operating this – at the time – brand-new type: 141 and 144 Filo, both of which were based at Mürted AB. Nominally assigned to the 1st Tactical Air Force and subjected to the control of NATO, these had nuclear strike as their primary role, but the THK used them for air defence purposes, also armed with AIM-9 Sidewinder air-to-air missiles. All were left in bare metal overall but had their wings painted in white and wore no other insignia but national markings, the 'last five' of their FY serials on the fin (62-12623 in this case) and buzz-numbers prefixed by FG. (Artwork by Tom Cooper)

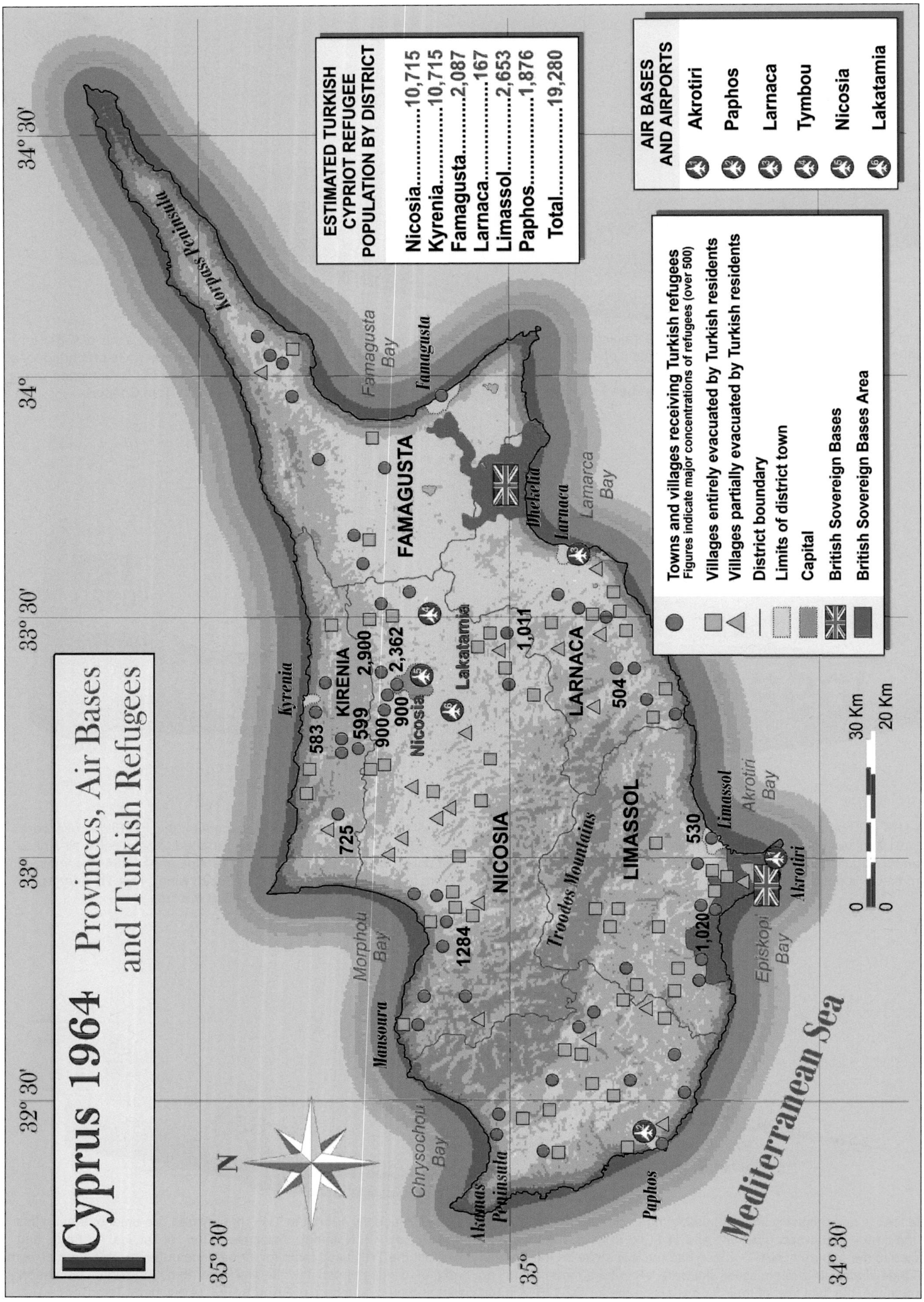

Cyprus 1964 Provinces, Air Bases and Turkish Refugees

N

Mağusa Peninsula

Korpass Peninsula

Famagusta Bay

Famagusta

FAMAGUSTA

Dhekelia

Larnaca Bay

Larnaca

Kyrenia

KIRENIA 2,900

599 900

583 2,362

900

Nicosia

Lakatamia

1,011

LARNACA

504

725

NICOSIA

1284

Troodos Mountains

530

LIMASSOL

1,020

Limassol

Akrotiri Bay

Akrotiri

Episkopi Bay

Morphou Bay

Mansoura

Chrysochou Bay

Akamas Peninsula

Paphos

Mediterranean Sea

ESTIMATED TURKISH CYPRIOT REFUGEE POPULATION BY DISTRICT

Nicosia................10,715
Kyrenia................10,715
Famagusta............2,087
Larnaca..................167
Limassol..............2,653
Paphos..................1,876
Total..................19,280

AIR BASES AND AIRPORTS

Akrotiri
Paphos
Larnaca
Tymbou
Nicosia
Lakatamia

Towns and villages receiving Turkish refugees
Figures indicate major concentrations of refugees (over 500)

Villages entirely evacuated by Turkish residents

Villages partially evacuated by Turkish residents

District boundary

Limits of district town

Capital

British Sovereign Bases

British Sovereign Bases Area

30 Km
20 Km
0

(Map by Anderson Subtil)

4
APHRODITE'S ISLAND

Cyprus is an island in eastern Mediterranean, stretching for about 220km (around 140 miles) from Cape Andreas in the north-east to the western extremity of the island and for about 90km (60 miles) at its maximum width (from Cape Kormakiti in the north to the Cape Gáta in the south). Much of the island is a flat, treeless plain called the *Mesaoria* ('between the mountains' in Greek), located in the interior and extending from the western to the eastern coasts. In the north and south this is bordered by mountain range;: the northern, the Kyrenia Range, is notable for its rocky, unbroken character and parallels the coastline, extending into the Karpas Peninsula. Its highest point is 1,019,m (3,343ft), The southern range, called the Troödos Mountains, is broken, has many abrupt cliffs and covers most of the south-western portion of the island. Its highest peak is Mount Olympus (1,951m/6,401ft). In the extreme northeast, the island narrows abruptly to form the Karpas Peninsula, which extends east towards the Syrian coast.

Cyprus has a typical Mediterranean climate, with hot and dry summers, and a cool, rainy season that extends from October to March. Average annual temperature is 21°C, while the average rainfall is less than 500mm. In antiquity, the island was famed for its extensive forests, but over the centuries the trees that once covered the central plain have been cut down for firewood, shipbuilding, and other construction, and much of the remaining forests were destroyed by fires that resulted from the armed conflicts of the 1967–1974 period. Centuries of deforestation have damaged the island's drainage system and no permanent rivers remain. Freshwater resources are also extremely limited as seawater contaminates the country's major aquifer and other sources are polluted by industrial waste and raw sewage. A number of watercourses bring the overflow from the winter rains down to the Mesaoria plain in spring but are dry most of the year. Nevertheless, there are two freshwater lakes and two large saltwater lakes.

Nowadays, forest growths of pine, cypress, and cedar cover about one-seventh of the total area, principally in the mountainous areas. Other indigenous trees include juniper, plane, oak, olive, and carob, while the eucalyptus has been planted extensively as an afforestation measure. Except for native and migration birds, there are few wild animals: mouflon and wild sheep are no longer common. The principal natural resource is arable land; the mountain soils tend to be peaty on higher flatlands, but are shallow and stony on the slopes. Farming provided income for much of the population until the second half of the twentieth century when the tourist industry and services became the key income generator. Other natural resources include copper, which used to be a major source of export earnings in ancient times, but mining has declined considerably in more recent times and was largely supplanted by agriculture, tourism and services as the main sources of income.

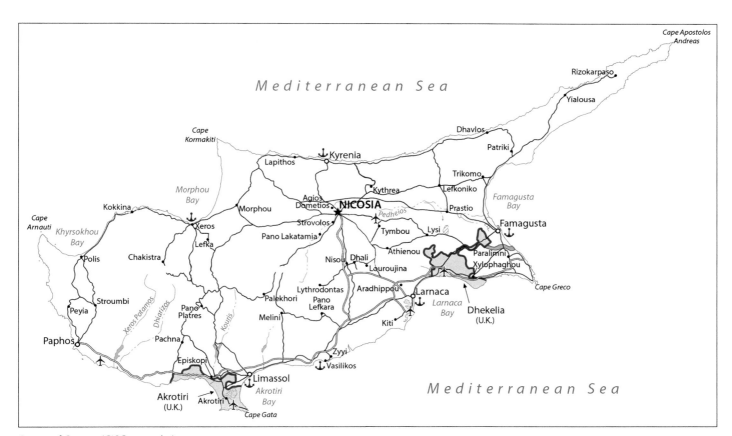

A map of Cyprus. (GISGeography)

History and Politics

According to archaeological investigations and conjecture, the aboriginal inhabitants of Cyprus were Indo-European people who had a written language. Extensive excavation has shown that during the Neolithic and Bronze ages, Cyprus had an advanced civilisation. The earliest confirmed site of human activity is Aetokremnos, situated on the southern coast and dates to around 10000 BCE. Water wells discovered by archaeologists in western Cyprus are believed to be among the oldest in the world. Approximately of the same age are a grave with a human body and an eight-months-old cat, dated to around 7500 BCE. Earliest attested reference to Cyprus was dated to the fifteenth century BCE, in Mycenaean. The recorded history of Cyprus continued with its partial occupation by Egypt around 1450 BCE, during the reign of Thutmose III.

Over the following centuries, seafaring and trading people from the Mediterranean set up scattered settlements along the coasts. The first Greek colony is believed to have been founded by traders from Arcadia about 1400 BCE – amid the first of two waves of Greek settlement. The second major wave of Greek settlement is believed to have taken place following the collapse of Mycenaean Greece, between 1100 and 1050 BCE. The Phoenicians began to colonise the island about 800 BCE but since the rise of Assyria around the same time, it was under the control of each of the empires that successively dominated the eastern Mediterranean; Egypt (around 550 BCE) and Persia (525 BCE, when there was the first recorded attempt to unify the city-states of Cyprus).

Alexander the Great took Cyprus in 333 BCE but after his death, the island again became an Egyptian possession. Rome gained control in 58 BCE, the East Roman Empire (the Byzantine Empire) took over in the year 286, and beginning in 649, the island endured repeated attacks by raiders from the Levant. In 1156, Raynald of Chatillon and Thoros II of Armenia brutally sacked Cyprus, looting and taking away so many of citizens and their possessions that the island took decades to recover. In 1185, Isaac Komneos, a member of the Byzantine imperial family, took over and declared an independent kingdom, but in 1191, Cyprus was seized by Richard I of England, who sold it to the Templar Knights. In turn, following a bloody revolt, the Templars sold Cyprus to Guy of Lusignan, titular king of Jerusalem.

The Lusignan dynasty built several large forts and castles (some of which are still standing), but was replaced by Venice, which formally annexed the island in 1489 and fortified it heavily. Following numerous raids through the fifteenth century, a full-scale invasion in 1570 – amid the Ottoman-Venetian War of 1570–1573 – brought Cyprus under the control of the Ottoman Empire. The Ottomans abolished the feudal and applied their *millet* system, under which non-Muslims were governed by their own religious authorities. Correspondingly, the head of the Church of Cyprus was invested as leader of the Cypriot Greek population and acted as mediator between it and the Ottoman authorities. This status ensured a special position of the Church of Cyprus and curbed constant encroachments of the Roman Catholic Church.

In general, relations between Christians and Muslims were relatively good during Ottoman rule but they had little direct contact in everyday life. This began to change in 1821, when the Greek War of Independence erupted; many Greek Cypriots left the island to join the uprising, prompting the Ottoman governor to arrest and execute hundreds. In turn, the first president of modern Greece, Ioannis Kapodistrias, called for union with the island – *enosis* – prompting armed uprisings both by Greek and Turkish Cypriots.

Following the Crimean War (1853–1856), the Russo-Turkish War (1877–1878) and the Congress of Berlin (1878), the Ottoman Empire leased Cyprus to the British Empire. The British took over the administration and developed a number of military bases – including the Famagusta harbour, which was a strategic outpost overlooking the Suez Canal and thus the route to India – along with other infrastructure projects and so initiated political reforms laying democratic foundations. However, *de jure*, Cyprus remained under the Ottoman sovereignty.

When the Ottoman Empire entered the First World War on the side of the Central Powers, London reacted with a formal annexation of Cyprus. Repeated offers to Athens were all turned down and eventually withdrawn by London. Similarly, following the First World War, and the subsequent Turkish War of Independence, when relations of neighbouring countries were regulated by the Treaty of Lausanne of 1923, the nascent Turkish republic relinquished any claim to Cyprus. London thus felt free, two years later, to declare the island a British crown colony.

Despite the establishment of the Legislative Council as a proto-parliament, under the British rule the relations between the Greek and Turkish Cypriots soured. Fearing a similar exodus like that of Cretan Turks after that island was united with Greece (in December 1913), the Turkish Cypriots saw themselves as a distinct ethnic group. That said, they were split over their future, some insisted on having a right to self-determination, while others favoured British dominance. Similarly, Greek Cypriots were divided between those seeing themselves as Greek first and hoping the British rule would lead to *enosis* and those who stressed their Cypriot identity, considered themselves distinct from the Greeks from Greece and preferred independence (although still feeling a part of the wider Greek nation).

In 1928, irredentists between Greek Cypriots refused to take part in the celebration of the 50th anniversary of British rule but Athens appealed for calm and limited the spread of anti-colonial articles in Greek Cypriot newspapers. On the other hand, the British decision to issue the Education Act – which sought to curtail Greek influence in the Cypriot school curricula – and the passage of a new penal code that, amongst others, granted the use of torture, continued causing political unrest. Rather unsurprisingly, a year later, Archbishop of Kition Nikodemos and Stavros Stavrinakis, two members of the Legislative Council of Greek Cypriots, issued a memorandum to London, demanding an *enosis* with Greece: London replied negatively.

October Events and the Emergence of EOKA

As tensions continued to grow, in September 1931, the British governor Ronald Storrs blocked a Legislative Council's decision to halt tax hikes that were to cover a budget deficit. Greek Cypriot members of the council reacted by resigning from their positions and in October of the same year, Archbishop of Kition Nikodemos called for his compatriots to engage in acts of civil disobedience until their demands for *enosis* were fulfilled. On 21 October 1931, a few days after London appointed a new governor, Greek Cypriot priests, city nobles and students organised a protest in Nicosia, which culminated in a siege of the Government House. After three hours of stone throwing, the protesters broke inside and set the building on fire before being dispersed by police. Protesting and rioting spread to the rest of the island and the order was restored only during early November, by when seven protesters had been killed, 30 injured, 10 were exiled for life and 2,606 received prison terms.

Although a nominally powerful signal of displeasure with the British rule, the so-called October Events badly damaged both the causes of the *enosis* and the Anglo-Hellenic relations. They prompted the British to abolish the Legislative Council and delegate the appointment of local authorities to their governor. All propagation of *enotic* ideas was strictly prohibited, as was any assembly of more than five people; Cyprus thus entered a period of British autocratic rule known as *Palmerokratia*. Unsurprisingly, the future of the island remained a matter of fierce disagreement, only temporarily subdued by the Second World War and then – during the Greek Civil War – with the fact that the struggle against Greek Communists was supported by London. However, no sooner was the latter affair over and in the light of repeated British rejections of their demands, irredentists between Greek Cypriots re-launched their activity. London reacted by restoring some degree of self-government but from the Greek Cypriot point of view, every time it did so, a true autonomy became an ever more distant ideal.

As of the 1950s, Cyprus had a population of about 520,000, of whom around 75 percent were Greeks. Although it had never been a part of modern Greece, Athens began claiming it for itself. Many of the Cypriot Greeks were in agreement. Correspondingly, they began organising armed resistance to British rule in form of the National Organisation of Cypriot Struggle (*Ethniki organosis Kyprio Agoniston*, EOKA). This came into being during secret talks with Archbishop Makarios in Athens of July 1952. As first, a 'Council of Revolution' was established, in March 1953 and from early 1954, shipments of weaponry to Cyprus began – at least with tacit knowledge of the Greek government. Ironically, EOKA never aimed to fight for independence, but for *enosis*.

Georgios Grivas, former officer of the Greek Army and veteran of the First and Second World Wars and the leader of the EOKA. (Dutch National Archives)

A group of EOKA insurgents; notable is the mix of civilian and military fatigues and a minimal collection of old carbines. (Albert Grandolini Collection)

Beginning in November 1954, it was led by Colonel Georgios Grivas, a Cypriot-born right-wing extremist, veteran of the Second World War and former officer of the Greek Army. It attracted support from the highly influential leader of the Church of Cyprus, Archbishop Makarios III. Initially, the insurgency was met with scepticism of the British administrators. However, once it initiated an armed struggle – on order from Makarios, and in form of coordinated bomb and grenade attacks on police stations, military installations and the homes of British officials – London reacted with intensive diplomatic manoeuvring and a counterinsurgency (COIN) campaign.

In similar fashion, like the British authorities and the majority of Greek Cypriots, Turkish Cypriots initially reacted cautiously, in part because the EOKA leadership at first pursued conciliatory politics towards them. However, in Ankara, the Turkish government announced it would not accept any change in the status quo of Cyprus that would be against its interests. Eventually, positions of the Turkish government prevailed and the leaders of the Turkish Cypriot community rejected an association with the insurgency.[1]

The Way to Independence

In March 1956, following unsuccessful negotiations and in the hope this might moderate the leadership of the Greek Cypriot community, the British deported Makarios to the Seychelles. Simultaneously, London contracted jurist Lord Radcliffe to develop a plan for self-government, but also launched a new COIN campaign involving around 30,000 troops. However, while the British Army was combing the insurgent bases in the mountains, Grivas managed to escape and the EOKA re-focused on urban areas, where it run hundreds of bombings and organised riots and strikes that lasted until March 1957, when the insurgent leader announced a unilateral ceasefire. Although temporary by nature, the truce enabled Grivas to re-focus the activities of his organisation on intimidation of the population and suppression on concurrent Greek Cypriot political groups.

To a degree, such activities were supported by the fact that while Turkish Cypriot leaders openly sided with the colonial authorities, many Greek Cypriots left the native police force – whether in solidarity with the EOKA or out of fear of reprisal attacks. Faithful to their usual 'divide and rule' policy, the British replaced them by growing numbers of Turkish Cypriots. In turn, starting in January 1957, EOKA began deliberately targeting and killing Turkish Cypriot police – with the aim of provoking unrest between this community and thus divert the British attention away from itself. When a Greek Cypriot was killed in the course of resulting protesting that escalated into riots, the Greek Cypriot leadership presented this as an 'act of Turkish aggression'.

Foremost, an unsurprising result was the growth of intercommunal violence as a result of which the British permitted the creation of separate Turkish Cypriot municipal councils, while the Turkish Cypriots began organising themselves into the Turkish Resistance Organisation (*Türk Mukavemet Teskilati*, TMT). Before long, the TMT was at war with EOKA which in March 1958, broke the truce with the British, prompting them into reacting with two additional, large-scale military offensives. That said, it was around this time that London has accepted its inability to suppress the EOKA and intensified the search for a way out of the crisis; indeed, a solution that would not embarrass Britain. For their part, Greek Cypriots became concerned about a partition of the island, while Greece was anxious of the crisis escalating into a war with Turkey. Correspondingly, in December 1958, Makarios was freed from his exile and a new round of negotiations arranged. The talks led to the London-Zürich Agreements of 19 February 1959; a compromise solution in which Cyprus was to become an independent and sovereign country, effective from 16 August 1960.

Treaties of London and Zürich

Along the constitution of the Republic of Cyprus, drafted under the London-Zürich Agreements, the population of Cyprus was divided into two communities based on ethnic origin – though in ignorance of the existence of other significant minorities, like those of the Gypsies and Maronites. The president was to be a Greek Cypriot, elected by the Greek Cypriots and the Vice President a Turkish Cypriot, elected by the Turkish Cypriots. The latter was granted the right of final veto on laws passed by the House of Representatives and on decisions of the ten-member government

British troops inspecting the locals during one of countless raids of what London termed the Cyprus Emergency. (Albert Grandolini Collection)

A trio of Chipmunk trainers from No. 114 Squadron, RAF, as seen on security patrol over the Kyrenia area, in 1959. (Albert Grandolini Collection)

(Council of Ministers), three of whom were to be Turkish Cypriots. In the House of Representatives, Turkish Cypriots were elected separately by their own community; the House had no power to modify the basic articles of the constitution in any respect and any other modifications required separate majorities of two-thirds of both the Greek Cypriot and Turkish Cypriot members. Similarly, any modifications of the Electoral Law and the adoption of any law relating to municipalities or any fiscal laws, required separate majorities of the Greek Cypriot and Turkish Cypriot members of the House. Overall, it was impossible for any representatives of one community to unilaterally pass any kind of bills and the numerically inferior Turkish Cypriot community could not be side-lined by Greek Cypriots.

Furthermore, representatives of Ankara, Athens and London signed additional Treaties of Guarantee and of Alliance, in which they specified that the Republic of Cyprus was to be an independent state maintaining neutrality on the international scene, while the three 'guarantor powers' (Greece, Turkey and Great Britain) promised to prohibit the promotion of either the union with any other state, or the partition of the island. In turn, they secured themselves the right to act in order to re-establish the state of affairs in regards to the bi-communal state, should the need arise. Correspondingly, Greece and Turkey were granted permission to maintain a small military presence – including a maximum of 950 Greek and 650 Turkish troops – 'necessary to train the Cypriot armed forces'. Moreover, Great Britain was granted possession of 99 square miles of the island for military purposes and access to a number of other military facilities around the island. Thus came into being, two 'sovereign base areas' (SBAs): one in the Dhekelia area, north of Larnaca in the east, and another south-west of Limassol, including an air base at Akrotiri, in the south.

In grand total, this made Cyprus 'not entirely independent' as its sovereignty was subject to external oversight and effective supervision – indeed, because it was giving both Greece and Turkey the right to intervene in Cypriot affairs – while the British kept large parts of the island under their control as military bases.

Population

The official census of December 1960 showed the population of Cyprus at 577,615, of which 104,350 (18.2 percent) were Turkish Cypriots, who mostly lived in small villages across the island, with relatively few in towns – Nicosia and its suburbs were by far the largest (22,134). Historically, this largely rural population worked the land and there was only a small middle class. Around 700 had benefitted from a university education and only 3,000 worked in manufacturing industries. Trade unions had mainly been segregated since the Second World War, with 49 Turkish trade unions brought together in the Federation of Cyprus Trade Unions (KTIBF). The leader of the Turkish Cypriot community and first Vice-President of the Republic of Cyprus was Dr Fazıl Küçük. He was born in Nicosia in 1906 and studied medicine at the Universities of Istanbul, Lausanne and Paris. In 1941, he founded the newspaper, *Halkın Sesi* (The Voice of the People) and then established the Cyprus National Turkish People's Party.

A group of Turkish Cypriot militants organised into the TMT. (Albert Grandolini Collection)

5
FACTOR FOREIGN BASES

Ironically, one of most important issues regarding Cyprus, but also Greece and Turkey from the 1960s and ever since, was that of foreign military bases on the soil of all three countries. Not only Britain, but the USA and then NATO, have constructed a large number of major military facilities in the area, the retention of which strongly influenced their politics vis-à-vis Cyprus; often to the point of dictating the same.

British Bases on Cyprus

The earliest foreign military bases in the area were the British ones on Cyprus. Developed systematically since the late nineteenth century, their importance grew by a magnitude with the withdrawal from Egypt and Iraq of the mid-1950s and with the island's proximity to the eastern edge of the Mediterranean, with the Suez Canal and the Middle East, they became of strategic importance as staging posts, as forward operating bases, and for training purposes.

During the EOKA insurgency, the RAF deployed Avro Shackleton maritime patrol aircraft from No. 42 Squadron on Cyprus, to patrol the surrounding waters and transport reinforcements.

Detachments of Gloster Meteor FR.Mk 9 reconnaissance jets from different units, flew occasional combat air patrols from Akrotiri and photo-reconnaissance of insurgent bases in the Trodos Mountains. The British Army operated Auster AOP.6 observation and liaison aircraft of No. 1910 Flight from Nicosia, Lakatami and Kermia, while in 1954, the Search and Rescue (SAR) Flight equipped with Sycamore HC.Mk 14 helicopters, was formed by the RAF at Nicosia. An additional unit, the Flight of the Internal Security Service, came into being in July 1955 and was equipped with Sycamore HR.Mk 14. That said, both aircraft and helicopters were used to limited extension, for example in support of British COIN operations Foxhunter, Pepperpot and Lucky Alphonse. In 1956, the Fleet Air Arm (FAA) of the Royal Navy had three Fairey Gannet AEW.Mk 1 airborne early warning aircraft from Naval Air Squadron (NAS) 847 forward deployed at Nicosia. They were busy tracking maritime movements and intercepting smugglings of arms by sea, but also by air, with the help of light transports used by the Greeks at night. Indeed, Gannets proved highly effective in this role, and guided a number of RAF fighters into interceptions of smuggling aircraft however, fighter pilots of the RAF never received an order to open fire.

During the tripartite aggression on Egypt in the course of the Suez War of 1956, the Royal Air Force deployed a reinforced wing of bombers, protected by multiple squadrons of fighters, photo-reconnaissance and ground attack aircraft at Akrotiri and Nicosia and a wing with six squadrons of transport aircraft at Tymbou. Moreover, a wing of French fighter-bombers and photo-reconnaissance jets was forward deployed at Akrotiri and a wing of transport aircraft at Tymbou. After this conflict, the government in London realised that its Middle East Command was unable to exercise effective control over forces deployed east of Suez. Correspondingly, this command node was split; what was east of Suez was controlled from Aden, which became the new HQ of the Middle East Command, while Cyprus became the headquarters of the newly-established Near East Command.

From 1957 to 1969, this node exercised the direct control over two SBAs:

- Akrotiri, with 41 square miles, and
- Dhekelia, with 58 square miles.

They were some 50 miles apart, both on the island's southern side. Except for the two major facilities, the British had retained 25 other sites across Cyprus, including radar units on Mounts Trodos and Olympus. They employed 8,000 civilians (including police), of whom about 70 percent were Greek Cypriots and 30 percent Turkish Cypriots. The British garrison usually included two infantry battalions, two or three squadrons of the RAF regiment, one armoured car squadron and a helicopter flight. These served for protection of not only, the two base areas, but also four RAF bomber units home-based at Akrotiri (Nos. 6, 32, 73 and 249 Squadrons) equipped with a total of around 40 English Electric Canberras, of which about 10 were equipped for reconnaissance. From 1961, Canberras received a nuclear strike capability and operationally, were meant to support both NATO and the Baghdad/CENTO Pact. For protection of the bombers, but also for training purposes, the RAF then deployed Thunderbird SAMs and a squadron of Gloster Javelin radar-equipped interceptors. Additional, regular detachments from units equipped with the then, brand-new, English Electric Lightning interceptor were also rotated to Akrotiri.

In 1963, London did consider abandoning its bases, but the conclusion was that: 'A British withdrawal from Cyprus would have profound consequences for our relationship within the NATO alliance. The island lies in a strategic position on the southern flank of NATO Europe, and it is of particular importance to NATO to avoid friction between Greece and NATO.'

The British were also concerned that the island might become communist-dominated, and withdrawal could add to nationalist pressures elsewhere. In 1964, the British Joint Intelligence Group on Cyprus examined the threats to the base areas from a Turkish or Greek intervention in Cyprus. These included Greek and Turkish Cypriots interrupting road communications, sabotage and local labour force disruption.[1] They planned to evacuate the 23,000 dependents living in the republic and a further 2,400 British citizens to the base areas under armed escort, given early radar warning of intervention. They would also declare Nicosia Airport as a British Protected Territory, denying its use to troops of either side. With remarkable foresight, they anticipated Turkish landings by sea and air in almost the exact places the Turks used in 1974.

US and NATO Bases in Greece

When Greece joined NATO, both the alliance and the USA rushed to construct a number of military facilities in the country. The most important US/NATO base in Greece became what was officially designated the Naval Support Activity Souda Bay (also 'Crete Naval Base'). This naturally-protected harbour on the northwest coast received a deep-water port capable of supporting the largest warships of the US Navy and in 1959, a major air base (subsequently expanded into a civilian airport). Both were under the control of NATO's Allied Naval Forces Southern Europe and then the Allied Maritime Command, but – as mentioned in Chapter 2 – were also used for military purposes by the Hellenic armed forces. Furthermore, in 1967, NATO established its Missile Firing Installation near the Souda Bay: an extensive range enabling live firing exercises. Combined, the three facilities converted the Souda Bay into the largest naval base in the eastern Mediterranean.

A view of the busy tarmac of RAF Akrotiri in the early 1970s. Visible is a pair each of McDonnell-Douglas F-4K Phantom II interceptors and Vickers Vulcan bombers. (Albert Grandolini Collection)

US and NATO Bases in Turkey

Turkey was only accepted into NATO after committing some of its best troops to the Korean War. This alignment with Western powers was based on a perceived common threat from the Soviet Union. The Ottoman Empire had fought a series of bitter wars against Imperial Russia and the new Turkish Republic faced Soviet pressure to establish bases on the Straits. Stalin claimed that the Montreux Convention of 1936, which governed the Turkish Straits, was biased against the Soviet Union and needed to be revised. He had also opposed the Soviet border agreement with Turkey regulated through the Treaty of Moscow 1921, as this conceded the Kars and Ardahan provinces. Therefore, he demanded border revisions. Throughout the Second World War, the Turkish government was more concerned about the Soviets than the Axis – which was a concern the Allied powers rarely understood. In 1944, when the Red Army reached the Turkish border with Bulgaria, its 37th Army appeared poised to invade Thrace.[2]

With hindsight, it appears likely that during the Moscow Conference in October 1944, Stalin used the positioning of the 37th Army to exert pressure on the British. There was still a lot of fighting to do in the Balkans and even the Red Army would need all the units at its disposal; thus a Soviet invasion of Turkey at that point in time was rather unlikely. However, Stalin threatened the Straits again in 1945, only to face firm British and US support for Turkey. In practice, Stalin had no intention of using force over the Straits, he was more focused on eastern Europe, where bases in Bulgaria achieved his security needs. That said, there is no denying that bringing Turkey into the Soviet sphere of influence would have been helpful for his position, it was just never 'important enough' to justify a war.

Meanwhile, the Americans became involved. During the Second Cairo Conference, in 1943, US President Franklin D. Roosevelt, British Prime Minister Winston Churchill and the Turkish President Ismet Inönü, reached an agreement for construction of an air base in Incirlik, outside Adana. For several reasons, the work only began in 1951, when a forward air base for recovery of medium and heavy bombers came into being at the site. Through the late 1940s and early 1950s, Turkey then moved closer to NATO and eventually, became a member and its membership was soon reflected in Ankara's foreign policy.

Turkey curbed its support for the Palestinians and supported Britain's position on the nationalisation of the Suez Canal, indeed, it warned the British Foreign Secretary that Egypt's President Nasser was an implacable enemy of the West and was trying to supplant Britain in Jordan and Libya.[3] In turn, Turkey's membership of NATO in 1952 was one of the arguments used by the British military for withdrawing from its bases in Egypt. Field Marshal Lord Alexander argued that Turkey's membership made a forward defence possible and maintaining the presence of 80,000 British troops in Egypt was no longer necessary. Turkey was also the only Muslim member of NATO and provided a key link to Islamic countries.

While its NATO role was important, Ankara had to balance competing security considerations regarding Greece and the Middle East. Turkey's geopolitical position gave it a vital strategic position in the alliance, but the emergence of the Middle East as the primary supplier of oil and gas added a new dimension. However, Turkey was far from the sources of arms and ammunition in the USA and Western Europe, while its topography divided its defences into separate theatres of operations, each having specific terrain features requiring different units, tactics and logistics. Rather unsurprisingly, Ankara thus became eager to obtain as much aid from the West as possible – which in turn, resulted in the rapid reform and re-equipment of its armed forces. Foreign bases were soon to follow.

The Military Facilities Agreement of late 1954, gave the USA the right to maintain around 24 military bases in Turkey. The Ankara complex included the Balgat Air Station, Esenboga Airport and communication installations. The Izmir complex included the Cigli Air Base, naval headquarters and facilities for communication and transportation. The Iskenderun complex (60 miles from Adana on the southeast coast), comprised a naval fuel depot and a cargo facility. The remaining sites were primarily related to communication and navigation, with some sharing with the Turkish Air Force and navy.

However, one of most important installations only came into being on basis of this agreement; this being the airfield initially known as Adana Air Base, but renamed Incirlik in 1958. It came under the main base of the 7216th Air Base Squadron, USAF and was then expanded to the level where it was used for the 'weather balloon' programme of launching reconnaissance missions over the USSR within the frame of Operation Gentrix. The CIA followed and from 1957, began staging its Lockheed U-2 operations through Incirlik, while over the following years, Boeing RB-47H Stratojets of the USAF and Martin P4M-1Q Mercator electronic intelligence-gathering aircraft of the US Navy, did the same whenever operating over the Black Sea.

During the Lebanon Crisis of 1958, the USAF deployed its Composite Air Strike Bravo – a force including F-100 Super Sabres, Martin B-57 Canberras, McDonnell RF-101 Voodoos, and Douglas B-66 Destroyer bombers – to Incirlik, expanded the facility into a major logistics hub and constructed an array of communications and signals intelligence-gathering stations on the surrounding mountains. Indicating its growing importance, by 1966, this base became the responsibility of the 39th Tactical Group USAF, which not only managed further expansion of support installations but hosted all US and NATO units rotated there.

Meanwhile, in 1952, the USA took over responsibilities for the Izmir Naval Base and a year later, the headquarters of the Allied Land Forces South-Eastern Europe was established in the city, followed with the HQ of the Allied Forces Southern Europe. To better facilitate the function of the local air base, this came under the control of the 7206th Air Base Squadron, USAF, in 1954. By 1962, the US and NATO further assumed responsibility for the Cigly AB and all the off-base installations in the Izmir area, constructed underground fuel tanks with concrete roofs, a fire-fighting system and a new energy supply system.

Political Price

In Greece and Turkey, a set of affairs from the late 1950s and early 1960s offers the best example of the effects and importance of foreign military bases on Cyprus. In 1958, the administration of the US President Dwight D. Eisenhower made the decision to deploy three squadrons with 45 PGM-19 Jupiter medium-range ballistic missiles in Europe. Originally developed as a successor for the US Army's PGM-11 Redstone, the Jupiter was a single-stage, liquid-powered weapon with a launch mass of almost 50 tons, capable of deploying a single warhead of 3.75Mt over a range of 2,400–2,700km (1,500–1,700 miles). It was the first nuclear-armed, medium-range ballistic missile operated by the USAF. When the French President Charles de Gaulle refused to accept their basing rights, Washington began searching for an alternative – and found it in Italy and Turkey. While two squadrons (each consisting of about 500 military personnel with 15 missiles) were deployed in the former, the third unit with 15 missiles, was deployed at five sites outside Cigli AB, near Izmir, starting in 1961. Both the missiles in Italy and those in Turkey were operated by the local air forces, but USAF personnel retained control over their warheads.

Both the Jupiters deployed in Italy and those in Greece, had not only Moscow but nearly all of western USSR and all of the Warsaw Pact countries within their range. Moreover, they were designed to be ready to launch within 15 minutes of receiving a corresponding order and their flight time over the maximum range was less than 10 minutes, leaving the Soviets little time to react. Unsurprisingly, their deployment became a hot topic for Moscow, where the Soviet leader Nikita Khrushchev complained: 'What would Americans think if the Soviets set up bases in Mexico or some other such place?'

Eventually, the US insistence on deploying Jupiters in Turkey prompted the Soviets into the Operation Anadyr – deployment of own nuclear weapons on Cuba, in 1962, which caused the Cuban Missile Crisis, perhaps the most dangerous crisis of the (First) Cold War. In turn, as part of a solution to this affair, the US President John F Kennedy 'privately' agreed to withdraw Jupiters from the Turkish territory. Rather unsurprisingly, this decision irritated Ankara. After all, the Turkish government had agreed to take the missiles when nearly all of NATO refused to accept them and the local political and military leadership regarded them as a matter of prestige at home and abroad. Indeed, the General Staff of the TSK concluded that they added significantly to its military power and was strongly against their withdrawal.

However, in the light of the Kennedy administration concluding the Jupiters were 'first-strike weapons' and also the fact that they were already obsolete and increasingly vulnerable to Soviet attacks, the Americans quietly withdrew them in April 1963. Instead, henceforth it was the responsibility of the US Navy to keep one of its nuclear-powered submarines equipped with Polaris intercontinental ballistic missiles (SSBN) on station in the eastern Mediterranean. Moreover, this affair became the principal reason for Turkey being donated its first batch of F-104G Starfighters armed with US-owned nuclear bombs.[4]

Apart from the case of Cyprus, military bases were a source of additional (and significant) income for host-countries, as well as a useful bargaining chip for their relations with the USA and Great Britain. At the same time, they were also a source of trouble – especially so in Turkey. The massive presence of the US military personnel and their dependants at multiple points caused considerable public unrest, eventually forcing Washington in 1963 to start drastically reducing their numbers. Nevertheless, neither Washington nor London ever had the idea to give up any of the facilities; on the contrary, their retention (and further expansion) became a matter of obsession, regardless of the circumstances and consequences. For example, when a series of 12 bomb-attacks repeatedly cut off the fresh water pipeline to Dhekelia on Cyprus, the British refused to give up and constructed a new water-supply system instead. They did vacate Nicosia and Tymbou in 1966, but only then due to the obvious pressures of space and continuously growing civilian air traffic.[5]

An emplacement for a Jupiter missile, together with its ground support equipment. Notably, the bottom third of the weapon was encased in a 'flower petal shelter', which opened prior to launch. The shelter was necessary to enable the ground crew to service the missile in all-weather conditions. (US Army)

The Incirlik Air Base, as seen from the air in 1987, by when a large number of hardened aircraft shelters were added to the existing facilities. (US DoD)

6

THE FIRST CYPRUS CRISIS

Generally, it was the Lausanne Treaty of 1923 that was the cornerstone of Turkish-Greek relations for most of the following 40 years. After the bitter war of 1919–1922 and tragic population transfers, it settled the boundaries of the two states, as well as Italy in the Dodecanese – and the UK mandate over Cyprus. However, many Turks felt the settlement conceded too much to Greece, particularly over western Thrace and over the Aegean islands that ring the coast of Turkey. Moreover, the diplomats who separated Greek and Turkish communities ignored the populations in Cyprus. Turkey was broadly content with British rule in Cyprus, reinforced by their treaty links to Britain.

After the Second World War, the Italian-occupied Dodecanese were ceded to Greece in the Paris Peace Treaty of 1947 rather than returned to Turkey. This reflected the ethnic makeup of the islands, but it raised serious concerns for the Turkish military. A 1955 Turkish book argued: 'Peace in the Middle East and security in Asia may be secured by the return of the Dodecanese islands to Turkey, since Rhodes can be used as a strong military base against Anatolia.'[1] Therefore, Ankara argued that Greece should not station troops on the islands, referencing the demilitarisation provisions of the 1947 Treaty,[2] while Greece claimed that Turkey was not part of the 1947 Treaty, and thus had no right to invoke it. This remains a sensitive issue between the two countries to the present day.

The cessation of the Dodecanese to Greece raised expectations for *enosis* amongst Greeks in Cyprus. Greek propaganda added to this expectation, although as the political campaign was primarily focused on the British as the colonial power, it rarely spilt over into conflict with the Turkish minority on the island. The Turkish government only became involved when Greece internationalised the issue at the UN, in 1964. Even then, at this stage the Turkish Armed Forces were more concerned about Rhodes with its military airfields than Cyprus. Both Greece and Turkey joined NATO in 1952 and in February 1953, Greece and Turkey signed a treaty of peace and friendship by forming the Balkan Pact with Yugoslavia, with a military element signed at Bled, in August 1954.

The 1955 London Conference was initiated to seek a solution to the growing dispute but achieved very little and angered Greek Cypriots because it acknowledged Turkey's role on the island. The Turkish government also sought to show it reflected public concern. This led to the Istanbul riots of 6–7 September 1955, organised by the ruling Democrat Party with the cooperation of Turkish security organisations, including the army's Tactical Mobilisation Group.[3] The demonstrations became out of control and enormous damage was caused to Greek property and churches. Between 13 and 37 people died and more than 1,000 were injured. Armenians and Jews were also harmed and similar riots occurred in Izmir. Many Greeks emigrated and between 1955–1960 in Istanbul alone, the Greek-speaking population decreased from 65,108 to 49,081.

The Zürich-London Agreements of 1959 brought independence to Cyprus on condition of forbidding *enosis*, but also the *taksim* – a partition of the island into Greek and Turkish portions (the precise aims of which were never clearly defined, even more so because Turkish Cypriot communities were spread all over the

island) – while safeguarding the security and rights of the Turkish minority. Precisely the latter issue became a major problem; generally, the Greek Cypriot community resented the constitution and the fact they had to share power with the Turkish minority, but also the denial of *enosis*. Unsurprisingly, they felt little loyalty to the new state. On the contrary, the majority of the Turkish Cypriots were ambivalent; although not delighted they were not part of Turkey but understood they had received a significant say in regards of power-sharing and were happy they did not end up in Greece.

Above all, many on both sides saw the creation of the Republic of Cyprus as a temporary solution, Greeks expected it to function until a suitable moment for *enosis*, while Turks were certain that if the country did move in that direction, Turkey would step in to divide it. Correspondingly, both *enosis* and *taksim* appeared as a serious alternative and on both sides, there were more than enough characters keen to influence affairs in one direction or the other.

Constitutional Crisis

The original Constitution of Cyprus was extremely complex. Essentially, it stipulated a strict separation of the two communities already down at the level of municipalities; the president was to be elected by the Greek Cypriots and the vice president by the Turkish Cypriots and both had veto rights over each other's decisions. The government was to be made up of seven Greek Cypriots and three Turkish Cypriots and the same ratio of 70:30 was to be applied in all other civil services, including the parliament and other authorities. Regardless of what level, all decisions required the consent of political representatives of both communities.

With most of the decision-making blocked quite soon after the independence, President Makarios opened negotiations with the aim of altering the constitution – supposedly with the aim of enabling smoother governance. However, at the same time, he became involved in organising a secret group consisting of prominent members of the Greek Cypriot community (including cabinet ministers and former members of the EOKA) which aimed to achieve *enosis* and began organising militants. Related efforts became known as the Akritas Plan (devised in 1963), and the organisation based on it became the Cyprus National Organisation (*Ethinki Organosi Kyprou*, EOK).

While it remains unclear how involved Makarios was in authorising the plan that envisaged replacing the Treaty of Guarantee with a plebiscite for *enosis*, he was at least aware of it – as were some of the Turkish Cypriots. Unsurprisingly, the president ran up against a wall. Ankara refused to agree and thus the Turkish Cypriots – who were informed about clandestine training of EOK militants in the Troödos Mountains, using weapons 'borrowed' from government armouries and considered the Akritas Plan as a blueprint for genocide – began making use of their veto powers over tax and other changes. Neither had a reason to trust a politician who – with interruption prior and during the release of Cyprus into independence – was all the time propagating *enosis*. The government of Prime Minister Konstantinos Karamanlis in Athens publicly abandoned the same goal in favour of Cypriot independence and then warned Makarios that any attempts to amend the constitution were not only likely to cause a break-down in Greco-Turkish relations but could even cause a war.[4]

Unimpressed, Makarios continued pushing and as soon as Karamanlis resigned and left Greece amid a spiralling political crisis caused by accusations of election fraud and assassination of a leftist member of parliament, in 1963, he began drafting a new constitution.

Despite repeated warnings from Athens and London, his list of 13 planned amendments was made public on 29 November of the same year. Ankara flatly rejected his plan, but for the leadership of Greek Cypriots, this made no difference. The rock began to roll.

Stillborn Cypriot Army[5]

According to the original Cypriot constitution, the republic was to remain strictly neutral on the international plan and to be protected by the National Guard, which was to boast exactly 2,000 officers and other ranks, all volunteers. These were meant to consist of 60 percent Greek Cypriots and 40 percent Turkish Cypriots and almost unnecessary to say, the majority was recruited from the ranks of the former EOKA and the TMT. For the purpose of training them, Greece was permitted to deploy a regiment-sized training group of 950 troops (*Elliniki Dynami Kyprou*, ELDYK or the Greek Cyprus Force, established on 20 November 1959 at Agios Stefanos, in Athens).

For similar purposes, Turkey deployed the 650-strong Turkish Treaty Regiment (*Kibrus Türk Kuvvetleri Alayı*, KTKA). Drawn from the 39th Infantry Division, the latter had four rifle companies and a heavy weapons company (with recoilless rifles 106mm calibre and 120mm mortars), a reconnaissance platoon, engineers, signals and other support units.[6] Initially, the ELDYK and KTKA were deployed close to each other, outside Nicosia. After the violence of 1964, the Turkish base was re-positioned to a sector north of the Cypriot capital, near the villages of Orta Keuy and Geunyeli, on the road to Kyrenia.

The training of Greek Cypriot and Turkish Cypriot troops was run separately and actually went nowhere – however, hardly anybody complained. While an amnesty for all of EOKA and TMT combatants was declared on independence, very few weapons were collected. Actually, neither of two organisations was ever obliged to disarm or disband and both largely remained operational. The Akritas Organisation/EOK assumed the tasks of the former Greek

Cypriot guerrilla and was smuggling arms to Cyprus in ever larger amounts. The TMT followed in similar fashion. The principal difference was that even without a national army officially coming into being, the EOK was operating with official permission of the Cypriot government, even if clandestinely, while all the Turkish Cypriot activities were 'illegal'. To make matters worse, several private militias of the Greek Cypriots emerged, most of which were operating at the discretion of their owners. The result was that, according to the US intelligence reports, by December 1963, both the Greek Cypriots and Turkish Cypriots had about 3,000 militants under arms.[7]

Although precise numbers remain obscure, there is little doubt about the flow of arms from Greece to the island, or that such efforts were clandestinely supported by different figures in the political and military scenery of Greece and that most of the arms smuggling was run by small vessels via the sea. However, it is at least 'likely' that submarines of the Royal Hellenic Navy also became involved in such operations. Furthermore, both officers of the ELDYK and numerous officers of the Greek Army specially seconded for this purpose, were deployed on Cyprus and became involved in military training of Greek Cypriots. For example, in January 1964, the British intelligence reported about the Greek Cypriot activities:

We have received a mass of evidence, some, the most significant, from the reliable sources, to show the Greek Cypriot paramilitary organisations in concert with the Greek Cypriot police alerted, issued with arms, and lectured on weapon handling and military tactics by officers of the Greek Army contingent, immediately prior to the outbreak of the fighting in December … We have received a number of reports which leave little doubt that both communities have been seeking and probably, although we have no confirmation, obtained additional supplies of arms from outside Cyprus.[8]

Greek Cypriot troops undergoing training in the early 1960s. (Albert Grandolini Collection)

Taken from a British helicopter, this photograph shows one of the improvised armoured vehicles of the Greek Cypriots, hidden under a shed and blankets, in the backyard of a private home in 1963. (Albert Grandolini Collection)

Cyprus Air Command

Within the frame of efforts to build up a national army, on 16 August 1950, the Makarios Government officially established a small flying arm. Initially, this included just two ground units: the 419th Air Base Protection Squadron, responsible for Lakatamia Air Base and the 420th Air Base Protection Squadron, responsible for Tymbou Air Base. In early 1964, the RHAF deployed a liaison team led by Lieutenant-Colonel Panagiotis Thomopoulos to Cyprus. This was first tasked with inspecting local airfields and reporting on their ability to support modern aircraft and then, with preparing support for any possible operations against a Turkish intervention.

Later commanded by Lieutenant-Colonel Nikolaos Tsintavis, the unit inspected the aircraft and helicopters of which in June 1964, was officially established as the 1st Air Squadron (also known as the 'Cyprus Flight' in Greece). Commanded by Captain Antonios Vogiatzakis, this included 12 pilots and 13 ground personnel and was equipped with a total of one Beech C-45, one Beechcraft 35 Bonanza, one Dornier Do.27A, one Stearman Model 75 (colloquially 'Boeing Stearman/Stearman'), two Piper PA-22 Colts, one Piper L-21B Cub, and one or two (sources differ) Agusta-Bell AB.47J helicopters. The majority of these were financed by private sources, while the Stearman was donated by the government of East Germany for crop-spraying purposes. Initially, it arrived in Greece in non-operational condition. However, it was put through an overhaul at the State Aircraft Factory and equipped with a camera taken from one of the RF-84Fs, before being flown by Lieutenant Athanasios Pritzios via Rhodes to Cyprus (in company of a RHAF C-47 for navigational aid as the Stearman had no navigational instruments). The sole C-45 (registration SX-EAB) was originally owned by the Hellenic Civilian Aviation Agency and used for calibration of navigational aids. After being replaced by a C-47, it was overhauled by the State Aircraft Factory, which exploited the opportunity to install a large camera bay and a system for target towing. It was coded as CR2 and deployed to Athalassa airfield on Cyprus by a crew consisting of 1st Lieutenant Menelaus Mantzavinatos, Captain Anastasios Karadimas and Master Sergeant Michael Pappas, who acted as flight engineer.

The principal task of the Cyprus Flight was irregular warfare; its pilots were trained to designate targets for RHAF fighter jets and to deploy (per hand) flares to illuminate targets by night. The 1st Air Squadron was home-based at Athalassa airfield, but frequently operated from any suitable roads and worked closely with the Cypriot Police. Its operations were coordinated by the Air Control Centre run by the RHAF detachment, which organised and ran it in form of a tactical air force headquarters. This command node included a photo-laboratory and interpretation department, responsible for processing photographs taken, not only by the Stearman, but also by the sole Bonanza. The secondary task was the preparation of local installations for landing, refuelling and re-arming of RHAF aircraft planned to strike any Turkish landing force and to create an early warning system that would report any kind of HVKK operations. For this purpose, the Cypriot Greeks obtained an old British-made radar from Greece and installed it on a hill top in the Kormakitis area, on the north-western tip of Cyprus. The unit operating this system was designated the 3rd Early Warning Radar station and was tasked with coordination of available air defences.[9]

In a similar fashion, the Greek Cypriots worked hard on creating an armoured force. By early 1964, the EOK already pressed several makeshift armoured vehicles into service, including two in Paphos, two in Famagusta, two in Nicosia and four in Limassol. It was also operating several patrol vessels, including three ex-German R-boats, left over from the times of the Second World War and purchased from a shipyard in Piraeus by a private sponsor. Two of the vehicles in question (P-01 *Arion* and P-02 *Phaethon*), were of the *R-151-*class and one (*Dedalos*) of the *R-218-*class and all were operated by officers and other ranks seconded from the Greek Navy. It is thus that, as soon as the crisis of 1963–1964 erupted, both sides were capable of putting thousands under arms, virtually 'over the night'.[10]

Turkish Resistance Organisation

As mentioned, it was in reaction to EOKA attacks – including explicit threats of a massacre published on 28 August 1955 – that the Turkish Cypriots organised themselves into the TMT. Officially at least, the organisation came into being in November 1957 with the aim of defending Turkish municipalities. The political wing of the TMT was directed by an Executive Committee based in Nicosia and led by Rauf R. Denktas, Kemal Tanrisevdi and Dr. Burhan Nalbantöglu. During the late 1950s, the organisation enjoyed the support of the government in Ankara and its military wing was directed by the General Staff TSK within frame of the Plan for Recoupement of Cyprus. For this purpose, Major-General Danis Karabelen was deployed to the island, whilst training camps with the capacity of up to 5,000 combatants, were established in Turkey. Early on, Karbabelen's most important aide was Lieutenant-Colonel Riza Vuruskan, a veteran of the Korean War, who acted as commander of the TMT and also administered the deployment of TSK officers on Cyprus. However, Voruskan was removed in the purge of special services that followed the 1961 coup, which resulted in the withdrawal of Turkish military support for the TMT; indeed, by 1962, some tensions developed between the TMT and the contemporary commander of the KTKA, Colonel Sunalp. In terms

of arms, between 1959 and April 1960, the TMT is known to have received 1,300 rifles, 300 sub-machine guns, 300 pistols and 40 Bren light machine guns.[11]

As the Makarios Government continued the build-up of the EOK, the Turkish Cypriot leaders and the TMT started their own contingency planning. They assumed attacks on Turkish communities would take a similar form to 1958. They planned to seal off Turkish quarters in towns from Greek mobs and fortify villages against Greek military patrols. Abductions and assassinations were to be met by reprisals in kind. The Turkish ambassador urged restraint, which frustrated Rauf Denktash. The new Turkish Prime Minister, Ismet Inönü, opposed unilateral attempts to change the constitution by either side and in discussions with the Greek government, appeared ready to make some concessions. The Greek government, for their part, cautioned Makarios against provoking the Turks. However, Makarios was encouraged by a change in government in Athens to press ahead with his constitutional change, which was rejected by the Turkish Cypriots and the Turkish government.

Bloody Christmas

As tensions grew, the EOK began the search for a pretext to attack, aiming for a swift knockout blow against the Turkish Cypriot community of Nicosia – which it hoped would result in the surrender of smaller enclaves. During the night from 20 to 21 December 1963, a car carrying weapons for Turkish Cypriots organised in the Omorfita (a district of Nicosia), was halted on a roadblock manned by the Greek Cypriot police. As the officers were inspecting the car and its passengers, an angry crowd of Turkish Cypriots assembled nearby. When the Greek Cypriots attempted to inspect a Turkish Cypriot woman, the situation spiralled out of control, resulting in

A militant of the TMT, armed with a Bren light machine gun, in position. (Albert Grandolini Collection)

exchange of fire in which one policeman and two Turkish Cypriots were killed. The news of the incident spread rapidly; in a matter of hours both Greek Cypriots and Turkish Cypriots began to mobilise their militants in Nicosia and the EOK attacked several Turkish Cypriot villages. Numerous exchanges of fire erupted all over the island, principally involving the use of personal weapons, but also bazooka launchers for rocket-propelled grenades and mortars. Whilest relatively few were killed, dozens were wounded.[12]

The constitutional order quickly fell apart. Although both President Makarios and the Executive Committee of the TMT issued calls for peace – and on 24 December 1963, both Athens and Ankara offered help in negotiations – the resulting ceasefire (which went into effect a day later), proved fragile, as there was no neutral body to control it. Moreover, not only were reports circulating about a massacre of Turkish women and children in Omorphia and the murder of patients in the Nicosia General Hospital, but the EOK attacked the strategically-positioned village of Agios Vasilios on the road connecting the capital with Myrtou, probably because it was positioned on a possible Turkish intervention route. A mass grave with 21 victims was subsequently discovered, with many bodies showing signs of torture. Moreover, Turkish Cypriot villagers of Mathiatis were driven from their homes (about 200 fled to nearby Turkish villages) and the EOK launched several attempts to seize the key pass linking the northern port of Kyrenia to Nicosia. The TMT fought off all these attacks, thus retaining the control over a key route for arrival of any help from Turkey, but – and at least as important – amid the violence, the mass of Turkish Cypriot government officials, civil servants, military and police officers either abandoned their posts, or were prohibited from reaching them. Thus, leaving the Greek Cypriots in full control of all official bodies and free to complain about a 'mutiny' of Turkish Cypriots.

Such acts provoked a profound change of mind in Ankara, where the government of Prime Minister Inönü decided to resume provision of aid to the TMT. Amid reports that up to 60 Turkish Cypriots were killed between 21 and 26 December, Vouskan was sent back to the island, followed by troops of the Turkish Land Forces infiltrated by fishing boats and submarines of the Turkish Navy. In a matter of days, the TMT boasted the strength of about 3,500, supplemented by 500 police officers, 150 troops of the token Cypriot Army, and around 13,000 civilians armed with firearms and improvised weapons. Moreover, F-100 fighter-bombers of the HVKK buzzed Nicosia, while a task force of the Turkish Navy approached Cyprus and remained in near the northern coast, from 23 to 25 December 1963.

Informed about this and similar developments within the EOK, London became concerned about the safety of its bases on Cyprus and attempted to mediate. The British proposed to Makarios that the UK, Greece and Turkey forces stationed in Cyprus, be placed under their command and they launched an effort to restore peace. The idea was accepted in luke-warm fashion, but the British persevered by creating the Joint Task Force (JTF). Nominally, this included 7,800 British, 1,000 Greek and 800 Turkish troops, under the command of Major-General Peter Young of the British Army. Actually, only around 2,500 British troops under Young's command became involved; they created a neutral zone between the Greek and Turkish sectors of Nicosia but left the TMT in control of Saint

Militants of the EOK undergoing training in one of several clandestine camps established around Cyprus in the early 1960s. (Albert Grandolini Collection)

Hilarion Castle above the pass connecting Nicosia and Kyrenia and did nothing when the KTKA moved out of its barracks to reinforce this position. In other words, the British were not trying to separate the combatants and their efforts came too little, too late. Moreover, Makarios continued to pour oil on the fire; on 31 December 1963, he publicly requested help from Moscow and upon receiving a positive reply, abrogated the Zürich-London Agreements.[13]

Emboldened, the EOK violated the ceasefire by additional attacks and although the UK, Greece and Turkey then arranged negotiations between Greek Cypriot and Turkish Cypriot representatives in London, about 150 people were killed by 15 January 1964, earning this affair the name 'Bloody Christmas'.[14]

The First US Intervention

The talks in London went on for weeks but bore no fruits. The Greek Cypriots were insistent on an abrogation of the Zürich-London Agreements, while the Turkish Cypriots declared the unified state as dead and demanded a federation, if not partition. At that point in time, the frustrated British government decided to get the US involved. This effort was successful as for the members of the Johnson Administration in Washington, it appeared 'natural' for the USA to become involve; Britain not only failed to mediate the crisis, but appeared unwilling to do so, while Cyprus was strategically important – both as a piece of real estate and an issue between two NATO members. Moreover, the Americans were concerned both about the possible influence of Greek Cypriot Communists, as well as Makarios' ties to Moscow and they preferred finding a solution within the Western military alliance, rather than via the UN. Therefore, President Johnson sent his emissary to run negotiations.

The result was a peace plan that included a complete removal of Greek and Turkish Armed Forces from Cyprus. This was promptly accepted by Ankara but Athens was reluctant and demanded conditions. Foremost, Makarios – exploiting a turmoil in Greek political landscape – rejected it; he was strictly against NATO involvement and expected to achieve his aims through the UN or the USSR. Unsurprisingly, Makarios' attempt to get the Soviets involved, and the fact that Moscow was backing the president of Cyprus, was a major agenda for Washington.

A group of Greek Cypriot militants with a Turkish flag captured during the Bloody Christmas period. (Albert Grandolini Collection)

Evacuation of 'captured' Turkish civilians from one of villages overrun by Greek Cypriot militants. (Albert Grandolini Collection)

Once again, US mediators prepared a new peace plan and this time, found agreement not only in Ankara but even in Athens,. However, Makarios only repeated his demands, while the EOK made its next move. On 21 January, it attacked Turkish Cypriot positions outside Paphos, provoking a clash that went on for three days and in which at least three Greek Cypriots were killed. Another, even bigger clash occurred on 6 and 7 February 1964 near Agios Sozemenos, leaving six Greek Cypriots and five Turkish Cypriots dead. Finally, 10 Turkish Cypriots were killed in Limassol on 11–13 February.

Meanwhile, both the EOK and TMT scrambled to obtain additional arms and continued mobilising able-bodied men under the age of 30 and organising them – principally into small units armed with personal weapons. Most of such Turkish Cypriot activities took place in the Kokkina area, the port of which was used to unload several arms shipments during January and February in 1964. Correspondingly, the EOK decided to focus its efforts on this region, at the next best opportunity.

The situation was also heating up in the skies over the Aegean Sea, as – starting in January 1964 – Turkish RF-84F reconnaissance jets flew a series of sorties over numerous islands in the Aegean and the Dodecanese. The Royall Hellenic Air Force reacted on 14 February 1964 by deploying a detachment of four F-86Ds from the 337th Mira to the Souda AB. They were tasked specifically with interception of Turkish aircraft in the Dodecanese area. Lieutenant-General (ret.) Konstantinos Chiou recalled:

> While in Souda, we were at 5 and 15-minutes alert, depending on daily tasking order and the tactical situation. We scrambled many times but we realised that the distance from Souda to Rhodes and Karpathos was large, and that in the case of an engagement we would have serious fuel problems. Especially the use of afterburner to increase speed and cut the range during interception was a big issue. Therefore, we were ordered to redeploy to Kasteli airfield, near Heraklion, which was slightly closer to the scene. When we scrambled from there, we have managed to detect some of intruders with our own radars. In turn, our intelligence was that the British had a very powerful radar on the Troödos Mountain of Cyprus, and that this was alerting Turkish pilots whenever we were approaching – because the Turks didn't have radar coverage over the north-west of their country.

Chiou's flight was back to its home-base by 11 March and replaced by another quartet of F-86Ds.[15]

A pair of Sabre interceptors of the RHAF seen in the process of scrambling. The activity of Turkish RF-84Fs over the Aegean of December 1963, kept the Greek interceptor units on near-constant alert. (PA)

A Greek pilot, with one of his squadron's F-86Ds. (PA)

Second Escalation

On 8 November 1963, the Enosi Kentrou political party, led by George Papandreou, won elections in Greece. A factor strongly contributing to this success was an intense anti-US propaganda campaign and a series of anti-American demonstrations both in Greece and Cyprus, in which President Johnson was blamed for siding with Turkey. Nevertheless, in February 1964, Washington turned to the new Greek prime minister with a request for help in convincing Makarios to accept the latest US peace plan.

While in agreement with some of US ideas, Papandreou had no interest in cooperating. On the contrary, he was meanwhile actively seeking for an abrogation of the Zürich-London Agreements, expecting this to help him achieve 'political glory'.[16] The unsurprising result was another standstill in negotiations. Sensing that the situation was spiralling out of control, in early March 1964, the governments of Cyprus and Great Britain referred the matter to the UN. On 4 March 1964, the UN Security Council (UNSC) issued a resolution calling for the Government of Cyprus to restore law and order and all members of the UN to refrain from the threat of the use of force.[17]

On 7 March 1964, aiming to revenge the EOK's sniping of their positions, a group of TMT militants opened fire into a crowd of unsuspecting civilians in the busy street of Paphos, killing 7 and wounding 34. Several houses in the Greek Quarter of the town were captured by Turkish Cypriots and over 200 Greeks taken hostages. In retaliation, the EOK reacted with all-out attacks on the Turkish quarter with the destruction of several mosques and there followed a week of hand-to-hand fighting. To bolster the garrison of Paphos, the CNG then deployed one of its newly-created battalions all the way from Nicosia. However, on the way in a south-western direction during the night from 8 to 9 March, this ran into a TMT-ambush outside Ktima and lost at least six combatants killed, in exchange for one Turkish Cypriot.

Outraged, the Greek Cypriots launched a new campaign of attacks, causing sufficient losses to prompt Ankara into issuing an ultimatum to Makarios; either the Greek Cypriots were to stop their attacks or Turkey would launch a military intervention. When the latter rejected, the General Staff of the Turkish Armed Forces ordered its forces into south-western Anatolia. At this point, not only did US President Johnson exercise severe pressure upon Ankara and Athens, but the UN also intervened. On 24 March, it authorised the appointment of a special mediator, Sakarai Tuomioja, from Finland, while three days later, it authorised the creation of the United Nations Peacekeeping Force in Cyprus (UNFICYP), with the task of 'preventing a recurrence of fighting' and to 'contribute to the maintenance and restoration of law and order and a return to normal conditions'.

In fact, the UNFICYP arrived with only minimal authorisations; its troops could only use weapons in self-defence, had a very limited freedom of movement and could not intervene to stop military personnel or weapons from moving around the island. Unsurprisingly, its effectiveness remained limited to defusing a few local disputes, but it could not stop the fighting. As the 6,411-strong UNFICYP – reinforced by some 175 civilian police officers – was deployed, the JTF was disbanded.

While this was continuing and as the scenery on both sides was meanwhile dominated by fanatics, the relations between the two communities on the island deteriorated to an irrecoverable level. On 25 April 1965, up to 1,500 Greek militants commanded by Vassos Lyssarides, attacked TMT positions around Saint Hilarion Castle, intending to capture the Kyrenia pass. The battle raged for three days until Makarios – under pressure from the UN – ordered a withdrawal. As a sign of victory, the TMT placed a huge Turkish flag on the peak 3,000ft/914m above Kyrenia.

Overall, while certainly well-meant, the UN intervention backfired as it recognised the Cypriot government – that now consisted entirely of Greek Cypriots – as the sole legitimate representative of the country. This was deeply resented by Turkish Cypriots who began to argue that any government without their involvement, was illegal.[18]

A British Army officer (left) chatting with his colleague from the UNFICYP. (Albert Grandolini Collection)

UN peacekeepers trying to separate Greek from Turkish Cypriot militants, in May 1964. (Albert Grandolini Collection)

Texans for Makarios

While the US and UN interventions of late March 1964 appeared to have brought the crisis to an end, tensions remained high. Indeed, through May there were ever more indications that it was moving towards boiling point. On 8 May 1964, British reported a reconnaissance flight over the Kokkina area that was 'almost certainly Greek'. However former RHAF RF-84F pilots denied that such a mission took place during May. These did not pass unobserved and on 14 May 1964, the HVKK 'returned the favour' by sending two RF-84Fs over Kokkina. A day later, another Turkish reconnaissance jet flew over Paphos and Nicosia. On 20 May, two other jets 'pressumed' to have been Turkish, overflew Paphos and Nicosia again, prompting bitter complaints in the Greek Cypriot press.[19]

By early June, it had been assessed that during the first five months of 1964, the TMT was reinforced by arms, food and ammunition delivered in more than 1,000 of small boats from Turkey. This enabled it to put 10,000 under arms and reinforce its defensive positions but it was under constant attack and facing shortages of food, medicine and water. The Greek Cypriot and the Greek governments decided that the time had come to launch a big offensive and achieve full control of the island.[20]

On 4 June 1964, the Makarios Government officially announced the formation of the CNG. Through the rest and during the following month, the nascent service was bolstered to between 25,000 and 30,000 under arms, with another 35,000 in reserve. To command them, the Makarios Government recalled George Grivas to Cyprus. Arguably, he was an arch-rival of the president but meanwhile wearing the rank of a general and as an 'implacable enemy of communism', he was expected to be both 'acceptable' to the USA and NATO governments and was the most suitable commander of the CNG. Furthermore, Athens decided to deploy an entire division of its army to Cyprus and began shipping these in small groups with the help of civilian ferries. By the end of August, their total number reached 957 officers and 7,238 other ranks.

The RHAF was also ordered to intensify its preparations. In response to Makarios' demands for combat aircraft, the Papandreou government ordered the air force to set up a small unit operating T-6G Texans (colloquially known as 'Harvards', regardless of their origin), and prepare for a deployment to Cyprus. Diogenes Harlaftis, then wearing a rank of a captain and serving as commander of one of training units at the RHAF Academy, recalled:

It was early July and I was at my farm in Stamata when my telephone rang and Colonel Sinouris, Deputy Commander of the Air Force Academy, ordered me to report at once in Tatoi. Once there, he informed me about formation of a training squadron, consisting of 10 Harvards, and briefed me on my new mission. I was assigned a commander of a flight of four; another flight was already forward deployed on Crete ... I gathered the pilots and ground crews, and briefed them – and especially our armament specialists – about weapons we were assigned. I personally checked the four Harvards and that every pilot had all the equipment necessary for our long-range flight, all the codes and radio frequencies ...

The unit gathered at the old Tatoi airfield (constructed in 1917) and began training by flying cross-country to Kopaida Lake, Biotia, Korinthos and back to Tatoi. When the time for weapons training arrived, this ran at the weapons range outside the Andravida AB. A single C-47 Dakota was equipped to support their operations and the transport was planned to deploy flash bombs to illuminate the target area. In Cyprus, this job was expected to be done by one of the Dorniers operated by the Cypriot National Guard. One of the fliers assigned to the unit, Brigadier-General (ret.) Vasilis Oikonomou, later recalled:

We began the conversion of our Harvards from training aircraft to warplanes. They had already installations for 2.75in and 5in unguided rockets, and hardpoints for bombs up to 250lbs under each wing. I do not recall if we ever used 500lbs bombs, but I do not think so. We also had to train to navigate in complete darkness while flying jut 50–100ft above

This old Valentine Mk II/III infantry tank from the Second World War, was modified into an armoured personnel carrier and pressed into service with the 7th Regular Group of the CNG in Limassol of April 1964. (Albert Grandolini Collection)

the ground, with help of map and stopwatch, and to fire these weapons under nocturnal conditions. It was not only difficult, but risky, too!

The training lasted two months, as recalled by Oikonomou:

One Sunday morning, the Chief of Staff RHAF, George Antonakos, called me to his office and told me that our mission was to defend Cyprus. He has promised the Prime Minister that the RHAF could handle any mission, from striking a raft to a destroyer. We were shocked: we didn't know what could happen if we had to strike a destroyer. But, it was our mission. We would do it no matter what we would face. We just never practiced anti-ship strikes. Instead, we were put on a 24-hour alert: five aircraft with six pilots, in two shifts.[21]

Apart from preparing Texans, the RHAF partially reconstructed the Kasteli airfield, outside Heraklion on Crete and began rotating a pair of 337th Mira's F-86D interceptors. Famous from the German airborne assault on Crete of 1941, this facility had not been in service ever since but received a fuel depot in 1964. As it was lacking a weapons storage, the jets arrived already armed and kept their armament on board throughout their stay there. Each was equipped with a pair of GAR-8s and a full load of 24 unguided rockets 2.75in (70mm) calibre. In early July 1964, the formation forward deployed to Kasteli and was led by Captain Chiou, who later recalled:

In summer 1964, our radar in Parnitha alerted us many times about unknown aircraft overflying Crete at high altitudes before turning east. Every time, our radar soon lost the track of them. Initially, we scrambled a pair of F-86Ds in attempt to catch and identify the mysterious intruders, but the problem was their high altitude. After several failed attempts, we re-deployed two jets to Souda AB … One day, the unknown aircraft appeared again, and a pair of Sabre Dogs led by Captain Ioannis Lazarou was scrambled. They rapidly reached the altitude of 30,000ft, and then used the zoom-climb manoeuvre to climb up to 40,000ft. Guided by the ground radar, they pointed their noses at the unknown aircraft and, soon enough, were able to catch with it. It was a British-operated Canberra.[22]

In those days, not only the usual Canberra bombers, but also Canberra PR.Mk 9 reconnaissance aircraft of the RAF, forward deployed on Cyprus and were underway almost everywhere over the eastern Mediterranean and much of the Middle East. The Greeks eventually identified the jet in question as belonging to the No. 73 Squadron – the same unit known to have once flown one of its Canberras along Greek RF-84Fs during one of NATO's exercises in Greece.[23] Later during the summer 1964, F-86Ds were also scrambled in reaction to Turkish reconnaissance flights over Rhodes. Although all the time operating at the limits of their operational range, in at least one case, they forced an RF-84F to abort its mission before reaching the island.

A T-6C/D Texan/Harvard of the RHAF, upgraded to the T-6G-standard, as seen in the mid-1950s. (PA)

A front view of the RF-84F of the 114 Filo, HVKK, with US FY-serial number 52-7450 (see colour section for additional details). Turkey operated a sizeable fleet of these reconnaissance fighters and they began operating over the Dodecanese and then over Cyprus, as soon as the crisis erupted, in December 1963. (Albert Grandolini Collection)

The Second US Intervention

Well-informed about Greek military preparations, US President Johnson continued negotiations with the Papandreou government, regardless both of its campaign of intense anti-American propaganda and a direct request to the State Department to help Greece achieve *enosis*. As the crisis was seriously threatening NATO and short of getting the Soviets involved, his demands were taken seriously. Numerous US officials became supportive of the idea of the union. Unsurprisingly, by early June it was the Turkish government that was disappointed. By that point in time, Ankara had acted in harmony with Washington, and accepted all US solutions without hesitations. However, concluding that its position in Cyprus was constantly worsening, on 4 June 1964, Prime Minister Ismet Inönü signalled to Johnson that as the USA were not willing to prevent *enosis*,

Turkey, 'decided to show that it is decisive to intervene on the island.' Fearing that an intervention was imminent, Johnson responded with an unusually strong answer, issued in form of a diplomatic note forwarded by the State Department and stating, between others, that, '... if unilateral Turkish action on the island invited a Soviet attack, then NATO was not obligated to defend Turkey'.[24]

Turkish Limits

Johnson's response, sometimes described as a 'diplomatic equivalent of an atomic bomb', was not the only reason for the government in Ankara to officially announce, on 5 June 1964, that it was abandoning the idea for a military intervention on Cyprus. At least as important was the lack of the military infra-structure necessary to support such an operation and uncertainties about the capabilities of its own armed forces. For example, contemporary US intelligence services assessed both Greece and Turkey as having the capability to alter the balance of military power on the island, however, the Americans concluded that the TSK was considerably superior, not only in numbers, but also in equipment, combat capabilities and because of the proximity of Cyprus to Anatolia. They concluded that the Turkish Land Forces of 350,000 outnumbered the Greek Army by more than three to one and in the case of a mobilisation, within 15 days, the Turks could expand their effective combat strength (by NATO standards) to 500,000 – or nearly double that of Greece. The Americans pointed out the excellent combat capability of the Turkish 39th Division and the fact that this was kept on alert and thus ready to intervene on the island on short notice. They assessed that neither side had sufficient amphibious warfare or airborne capacities and that the Hellenic Navy was, 'generally superior' to the Turkish, but expected it to prove extremely vulnerable if trying to operate in the Cyprus area – both because of the large HVKK and due to the Turkish superiority in submarines. In this regard, they further concluded that the HVKK was superior to the RHAF with a 'fairly proficient fighter-bomber force' and also because of its equipment with F-100s and F-104s. The mass of these were home-based within striking distance of Cyprus and could reach back upon significant stockpiles of ammunition on bases in southern Anatolia.

For comparison, the US intelligence concluded, the Greeks had only recently received their first F-104s, were not yet proficient on them and would have experienced 'great difficulties' if trying to operate in the Cyprus area. Finally, while concluding that both the Greek and Turkish Armed Forces had deficiencies in logistics support, communications equipment and combat vehicles, they foremost assessed that it would be the issue of reserves in ammunition that would result in a short, rather than protracted, conflict.[25]

In fact, the creation of the Republic of Cyprus brought a new state actor into the Turkish military calculations. Indeed, it can be said that it caught the government in Ankara and its armed forces, entirely unprepared. Therefore, while looking formidable on paper, as of 1964, the TSK was ill-positioned for deployment on Cyprus. All the US and NATO aid went into creation of a strong conventional army, trained, equipped and organised to fight the USSR and the Warsaw Pact. Correspondingly, principal formations of the Turkish Army were all deployed either along the borders to Bulgaria, or those to the USSR. Indeed, as of the time, the General Staff of the TSK had no plan for an invasion of Cyprus. Furthermore, the air force was relatively large and well-trained, but largely equipped with aircraft meanwhile considered obsolete. Until arrival of F-104G Starfighters, in late 1963, the HVKK had only three fighter units that could be considered 'modern' – all flying F-100Ds. The rest of the force consisted of decade-old and growingly troublesome F-84Gs and F-86s, while many of the second-hand F-84Fs handed down from NATO members, were in poor condition. The air transport capability consisted of five C-47-units but only a handful of helicopters. Under best circumstances, these could airlift about a battalion of troops on one day. Arguably, the army aviation meanwhile operated up to 150 Piper L-18/L-21 Cubs, but these could not carry more than two passengers each. The navy was in no better position; not only did it not operate any aircraft nor helicopters and had next to no amphibious warfare capability, but most of its warships were simply old and in need of modernisation or even replacement.

At least as important was the factor of logistics; as of the early 1960s and except for US/NATO-facilities in the Izmir area, the southern coast of Anatolia was seriously under-developed. There was no modern road along the coast from Antalya to Mersin (this was only constructed in the 1970s) and no road connecting Antalya and Izmir (constructed only in the 1980s). In fact, the whole Turkish coast opposite Cyprus, was devoid of any kind of military installations between Izmir in the west and Mersin in the east. There were no air bases, not a single radar station operated by the HVKK (at least not between Izmir and Mersin) and only the civilian airport at Adana and the US/NATO base in Incirlik, the Turkish part of which could only support F-100 fighter-bombers. The other military airfield existing as of 1964 in this part of Turkey, was Konya, but this was still a secondary installation and it would take at least a year to expand it into a full air base. Therefore, the nearest existing and active air base – Erhac AB, near Malatya – was actually, too far away and housed only a single F-100-squadron.[26]

While all such considerations might not have mattered much to Makarios, Papandreou or their military commanders (not to mention the Greek public), all of whom never stopped complaining about Turkish aggression and intentions to launch an invasion, generals in Ankara and Istanbul quickly concluded that it would require much more than 'maximum effort' for their already overstretched forces to run any kind of a serious operation on Cyprus. Therefore, the decision of Inönü's government was actually of domestic and military nature, and only partially influenced by Johnson's intervention.

7
ON THE BRINK OF WAR

Throughout June 1964, US President Johnson continued to try negotiating with Papandreou. Meanwhile, the essence of his message was 'negotiations or Turkish military intervention' – although never as threatening as his message to Inönü from early June. However, after six months of crisis, the Greek prime minister became convinced that Ankara and Washington were bluffing, that the USA would never let Turkey deploy troops on Cyprus and thus, the advantage was on his side. Therefore, he rejected not only overt US offers for mediation (Acheson Plan), but even Johnson's offers for secret negotiations. Makarios seems to have followed in fashion, even more so because he felt firmly in control; not only had Cypriot Greeks established themselves in complete control over the Cypriot government, but they became determined to achieve full control over the island. With hindsight, it can be said that from that point onwards, any kind of a peaceful settlement became nearly impossible.

The TMT of Summer 1964

By July 1964, the TMT was reasonably well-organised but its forces were scattered all over Cyprus. Its primary problem being that many Turkish Cypriots lived in mixed communities, not only in isolated villages. The chain of command was led by Rauf Denktash, meanwhile based in Ankara, via the commander of the KTKA and the commander of the TMT, who by then was Sami Omer Djoshar. It included five town commands (Nicosia, Famagusta, Larnaca, Limassol and Paphos), all of which were run by TSK officers (mostly Colonels and Majors, though often described as 'Brigade-Majors'). Some oversight of this complex force was exercised by the Turkish Cypriot Minister of Defence, Osman Erek. Military units of the TMT typically had around 300 effectives, each with four departments (or 'Direks' in the local parlance, which stood for Pillars):

- Direk I: personnel
- Direk II: intelligence & security
- Direk III: operations, planning and training
- Direk IV: administration.

Full-time combatants were paid and discipline was strict, with any disappearance being punished by imprisonment or beatings. Part-time combatants were rostered to perform guard duties and attended monthly training sessions. The KTKA, which used to provide minimal support at earlier times, meanwhile deployed officers to instruct TMT units in isolated areas, although there were limited opportunities for live firing exercises and critical ammunition shortages. As a result, most of the Turkish Cypriot troops were trained for static defence only, although there were some mobile units in the Nicosia area. Most important of the latter was a commando unit based in Hilarion area, which was also trained in mountain warfare. Female combatants took part in parades held in the Nicosia area, but only some 200 out of potential 7,500 women were enlisted due to shortages of arms and equipment (especially communication systems, most of which were stolen British field telephones). Only the headquarters of the TMT in Nicosia and Hilarion had effective radio links with Ankara, while the Turkish Embassy had secure communications. A strict communication security was enforced and codes and cyphers were widely used.[1]

Each of the units consisted of three rifle companies (each including three platoons, with light machine gun teams and bazookas) and a support platoon with mortars and bazookas. While the military organisation was reasonably good, medical facilities were minimal and largely dependent on civilian resources. British intelligence estimates from 1966 were quoting deliveries of up to 16,000 firearms of all calibres, including 8,000 (mostly British) rifles .303 calibre, 1,700 Sten and Thompson sub-machine guns, 3,000 pistols, 3,500 shotguns and 300 light machine guns (primarily Brens and Brownings). Moreover, the TMT should have received 120 light, 40 medium and 10 heavy mortars, 100 recoilless rifles and bazookas. However, there was little ammunition for all of this (about a week's worth at most) and only a handful of improvised artillery pieces and armoured vehicles. Actually, the command of the Turkish Cypriots always counted on Turkish air superiority to cover its shortage of heavy weapons.

Table 6: Turkish Forces in Cyprus, June-August 1964

Wing	Squadron
TMT	
infiltrators	500
volunteers	2,000
conscripts	2,500
part-time	10,500
police	1,500
total	17,000

KTKA	650
other Turkish combatants	500
reserves	4,000
civil defence	7,000
Total	**27,500**

Table 7: TMT Deployment by Enclave, June-August 1964

Wing	Squadron
Nicosia/Hilarion	6,850
Famagusta	3,200
Larnaca	1,850
Limassol	1,400
Lefka	1,450
Kokkina	450
Paphos	1,800

August Offensive

Apart from the connection from the port of Kyrenia to Nicosia, the second most important sector protected by the TMT was a system of defensive positions on the 667-metres-high Mount Lorovonous, near the north-western coast of Cyprus and overlooking the port of Kokkina. Grivas and his staff concluded that the TMT was in the process of setting up a bridgehead for a Turkish invasion in this area and – under the pretext of the Turkish Cypriot position cutting off numerous Greek villages from the outside world – set in motion a major campaign to recover the elevation. By 6 August, the 12th Tactical Group of the CNG was in position. This comprised the 206th Infantry Battalion, the 31st Ranger Squadron and a few minor scout and artillery units. The attack was initiated early on 8 August with CNG units simultaneously advancing in three directions; from the western side along the coast on Kokkina; from the east on Mansoura and from the south on Lorovonous Mountain. Artillery of the Greek Army division that was in still in the process of deploying on Cyprus, supported this assault – while the UNFICYP took no action.

Unsurprisingly, the offensive and the reported death of 25 Turkish Cypriots, promptly set off alarm bells in Ankara; upon receiving reports about a 'major' assault on Lorovonous, the government in Ankara was de facto cornered. By then, it had threatened an intervention three times but did not act in response to the Bloody Christmas events, nor in reaction to attacks of March and June. But now, a military intervention was a matter of its political survival – as much as that of Turkish Cypriots, even more so as, gauging by the ferocity of the Greek Cypriot assault, the Turkish intelligence quickly came to the conclusion that 'Athens' (in the sense of the Greek armed forces) was directly involved. Therefore, Turkish President Cemal Gürsel ordered the General Staff to mobilise the TSK and send it into action. The sole means immediately on hand was the air power, in form of the HVKK.[2]

Turkish Intervention

After several hours of re-deploying combat aircraft to Adana and Incirlik and then bombing them and briefing their pilots, the Turkish Air Force went into action during the afternoon of 8 August 1964. Around 17.00hrs, as the battle for Kokkina was in full swing, the first two F-100C Super Sabre fighter-bombers from the 111th, appeared high in the sky, before diving down to make two bombing and strafing passes each. Additional quartets of HVKK F-100s from the 111 Filo, reinforced by several from the 181st Filo followed and later on, even a fourship of F-84Gs from the 191 Filo flew one attack mission. The primary target of air strikes were CNG positions around the village of Kato Pyrgos and nearby hills from

One of two Daimler Dingos of the CNG seen next to an improvised armoured vehicle based on a bulldozer, with a British Army APC in the rear. (Albert Grandolini Collection)

A front view of one of the bulldozers converted into improvised armoured vehicles for the CNG, as seen during the fighting in summer 1964. (Albert Grandolini Collection)

The Greek Cypriot assault on Turkish Cypriot positions in the Lorovonous area began with an advance of Marmon-Herrington armoured cars and other armoured vehicles of the CNG. Unexpectedly, these ran into TMT militants armed with recoilless guns, which quickly knocked out a number of Greek Cypriot 'tanks'. (Albert Grandolini Collection)

which Greek Cypriot spotters directed artillery fire using radios. All of these were heavily hit by a combination of BLU-1B napalm tanks, AN/M64A1 and M117 general purpose, high-explosive bombs (500lbs/250kg and 820lbs/372kg, respectively) and 20mm internal guns.

As air strikes on CNG positions went on, a formation of F-100s led by Major Hüssenyin Capaoglu spotted the R-boat *Phaethon* of the CNG underway off the coast of Gemokonagi, about 25km east of Mansoura and attacked. The vessel commenced evasive manoeuvres and returned fire by its 20mm anti-aircraft gun but received multiple hits into the engine compartment that exploded, killing seven of the crew. The four survivors then piloted the burning wreck on the ground next to Kokkina, where it was abandoned while engulfed in flames. Minutes later, another F-100-formation appeared, led by Captain Cengiz Töpel, to spot the Cypriot gunboat *Arion*, further up the coast and moving in direction of Kokkina. The vessel was strafed by gun fire but managed to avoid the worst of it. In turn, its crew claimed the lead Super Sabre shot down by the fire of its 40mm Bofors anti-aircraft gun. The pilot was forced to eject.[3]

According to contemporary British and Turkish reports, Captain Töpel was captured, but then tortured and burned alive by Greek Cypriots. According to Greek accounts, he was badly wounded by a combination of ejecting at critically low altitude and ground fire but recovered from the sea. Captain Kalenterides and Captain Tsertos of the CNG then flew him with the AB.47G helicopter to a hospital. Kalenterides commented:

> When I went to the intensive care unit of the hospital, I wore a medical shirt and questioned the prisoner in English. He did not answer. When I asked him in Turkish, what was his mission, he told me he took off from Eskisehir and his primary target was Cyprus, but the secondary was Souda Air Base on Crete. His statement was confirmed by the two flight plans that were removed from his flight suit. A few hours later, the pilot died in the hospital because of his serious wounds.

An examination of Töpel's body by Danish specialists on behalf of the UN and their report, were rather damning for the Greek Cypriots in their conclusions.[4]

This dramatic photograph shows one of CNG's patrol boats under attack by one of F-100s from Major Capaoglu's formation, late in the afternoon of 8 August 1963, off the coast of Mansoura. (Ole Niklajsen Collection)

on this unusual mission; their actual task was that of 'showing the flag', making low altitude, high speed passes over CNG positions, to bolster the morale of its combatants.

While approaching Cyprus, Captain Louloudakis attempted to contact the RHAF detachment deployed on the island but received no reply. Thus, once over the Morfou area, the jets descended, preparing for their passes. At that point in time, Louloudakis realised that one of his drop tanks was not transferring fuel. While going through his checklist, he did everything possible to solve the problem, but to no avail. Knowing the formation was about to accelerate to 450 knots per hour and drop tanks were best jettisoned at just 250, he ordered 1st Lieutenant Theodoropoulos to go ahead and complete the mission at high speed and low altitude over Nicosia, while he and his Number 2 were to head for the village of Mansoura, which was much closer. The formation split into two pairs shortly before passing north of Akrotiri; around the same time, pilots tuned their radio receivers onto the Cyprus Public Radio station (PIK), to hear latest news 'from the front'. Their presence soon became known as the PIK reported that RHAF jets were airborne over the island. As they descended to low altitude, they could see civilians coming out to hail them and wave – everybody was engraved in emotions. Unknown to the pilots was the fact that the communications between Greece and Cyprus were so poor that the Cypriot National Guard was never informed about the arrival of RHAF aircraft. Thus, its troops opened fire at them, but missed.

After two passes each over Nicosia and Mansoura, the four F-84Fs made a turn back in direction of Greece. Captain Louloudakis' element took a course towards Rhodes, which was much closer. Once over the sea, the formation leader slowed down to 250 knots and managed to jettison both of his drop tanks. Climbing to 25,000ft, he could clearly see the island ahead of him but had forgotten to call the local tower to turn on the runway lights and thus decided to continue for Kasteli.[8] After establishing contact with the tower, he declared an emergency due to fuel shortage and a faulty drop tank. Just before reaching the coast of Crete, fuel warning lights came up

but to his amazement, the engine was still running. First Lieutenant Tremoulis flew on his wing, ready to provide position in the case the leader would be forced to eject. Eventually, Louloudakis lined up with the runway, pulled his throttle back to idle position and glided his F-84F to a straight in approach over the mountains. He managed to land safely; the engine stopped as he was clearing the runway. The last he did was to call Tremoulis about his fuel state: since this was still at 1,500lbs, he ordered him to continue for Souda. Many years later, the Greek flight-leader recalled: When I cleared the runway, my engine stopped due to fuel shortage. I saw the ground crews come to my aid and was thinking about smashing my head against the canopy: I never came to the idea to fire my machine guns and thus lighten up the weight of my jet … '[9]

Cooldown

The second of the 'last minute' decisions by the Greek government in Athens not to become directly involved or initiate open hostilities against Turkey, almost caused a melt-down in its relations with the Greek Cypriot authorities and the National Guard. The disagreements reached a point where Grivas left Cyprus, while the Chief-of-Staff CNG, Lieutenant-General Karagiannis, resigned from his position. Makarios appointed Lieutenant-General Ilias Prokos instead and publicly demanded military assistance from the United Arab Republic (Egypt) and the Soviet Union. Certainly enough, the Soviet Premier Nikita Krushchev did not miss the chance to express his 'support for Cyprus and its people', but whilst being worrying for Washington, his reaction remained limited. Eventually, it was Papandreou who stepped back under US pressure and returned to negotiations; on 10 August 1964, Athens, Nicosia and Ankara agreed a new ceasefire and engaged in a new round of negotiations in Geneva. These went for weeks and – between others – included a solution in the form of offering the Karpas Peninsula to Turkey for 50 years in exchange for *enosis*. Amid severe differences between Papandreou and Makarios, no agreement was found and Greece withdrew its forces from the 6th ATAF and other NATO command

In August 1964, the RHAF put at least six F-84Fs of the 338 Mira – one from its sister 339 Mira is visible on this rare air-to-air photograph – on alert for possible missions to Cyprus. However, fuel calculations have shown that when loaded with a pair of drop tanks and bombs each, plus four unguided rockets, the jets could not reach the island, fight and still return to Crete. Therefore, pilots were given the options of continuing for Lebanon and either landing or bailing out there or ejecting over the RAF Akrotiri. Apparently, most considered the latter. Ultimately, this mission was scrapped before it was launched. (PA)

node but although the USA agreed to the presence of Greek Army troops on the island, the CNG withdrew from frontal confrontations with the TMT and the ceasefire held.

Tensions in the air and on the ground remained high, nevertheless. During the night from 10 to 11 August 1964, reports reached Nicosia that a group of four destroyers from the Turkish Navy were in the process of approaching Cyprus from the north. By the morning, they could be clearly seen from Mount Lorovouno, especially as two of them approached the Kokkina area to less than 1,000 metres and then started unloading crates onto several smaller vessels, while recovering wounded combatants of the TMT. The warships received plentiful support from F-100s of the HVKK, which were almost constantly airborne over Cyprus, even if no additional air strikes were flown; Ankara thus signalled its respect for the ceasefire. Despite Turkish fighter jets above him, Vogiatzakis took off in his Do.27A again, this time with Major-General Voutsinas on his side and flew reconnaissance from Mount Lorovouno to the village of Mansoura, where he sighted groups of Turkish combatants and wounded on the beach, apparently waiting to be embarked to one of warships off the coast.[10]

Thunderflashes over Cyprus

By that point in time, only the RF-84F Thunderflash reconnaissance fighters of the Turkish Air Force were operating over Cyprus; those of the RHAF never ventured anywhere near the island. This changed at around 09.00hrs of 16 August 1964, when the Ministry of Defence in Athens ordered the deployment of six jets from the 348th Mira to Souda AB, in preparation for a mission to Cyprus. This call took the unit by surprise as it was not yet fully operational and some of the pilots involved, were underway on training sorties. The latter was even more important as, although some claimed that involved pilots were selected within the squadron, actually, all were picked by the HQ of the RHAF: they included Major Efthimios Roulias with Lieutenant Theophanes Demopoulos on his wing, with Lieutenants Nikolaos Papadopoulos, Stavros Danias, Ioannis Pritzios, and Sergios Papasis.[11]

While pilots were briefed, around 12.00hrs, a C-47 carrying ground personnel, spares and photographic equipment, took off in the direction of Crete. The principal issues were what to do if they were to be intercepted by RAF Lightings from Akrotiri or by Turkish fighters, also the lack of tactical pilotage charts. One hour later, the first three RF-84Fs – led by Major Roulias – became airborne, followed by the other three, led by 1st Lieutenant Demopoulos. On the ground in Souda, all jets were equipped with JATO bottles and pilots received another briefing: they were to approach Cyprus at an altitude of 28,000ft, but photograph their targets from about 10,000ft, using vertical cameras. Each jet was fully refuelled and carried the full load of ammunition for four internally installed 12.7mm machine guns; this was necessary as not only had they to reach Cyprus but actually fly well over it and they needed a reserve in case of an aerial engagement.

The following morning, on 17 August 1964, six Thunderflashes launched, in strict radio silence and with two to five minutes separation. As usual, they were routed over Rhodes, where Papadopoulos' jet developed a problem with drop tanks, forcing him to abort and return back to Souda. On reaching the western coast of Cyprus, they began descending towards their targets. Heading for Morfou, Pritzios was in the process of descending to 10,000ft, when he saw two unknown fighters approaching from his left and right. He could not identify them immediately but took no evasive action and only increased his speed. He reached his target, took photographs and returned to Rhodes for refuelling, before flying back to Souda.

Tasked with photographing Kyrenia, Roulias experienced a similar situation; while descending, he was intercepted by a pair of RAF Lightnings. Their pilots signalled him to clear the area, but the pilot ignored them and pressed on. The British then approached and flew in front of his jet, to cause turbulences and thus cause his jet to shake. Nevertheless, Roulias continued and managed to take his photographs before returning straight to Crete. Much to his disappointment, it turned out that the British tactic was successful and all of his reconnaissance photographs were blurred by vibrations.

Dranias was over Morfou when he heard Roulias' warning about the presence of unknown fighters. Only seconds later, he saw two jets approaching him, jettisoned his drop tanks and withdrew after making a 180-degree turn. The last two RF-84Fs were flying well behind him. Demopoulos was intercepted by Lightings before reaching the coast but he ignored their signals to break, noted their serial numbers and pressed on. Finally, Papasis was intercepted by the same pair of British jets:

There were two Lightings, one coming from my left and the other from my right. Their tails were painted black with yellow stripes and one had the number 110 on his fin. They signalled me with their hands to leave the airspace over Cyprus, but I continued towards my target, Agios Ilarionas, while descending to 10,000ft. Then the right Lighting broke off, pulled high and took position above and behind me, like if he would open fire. The other remained on my left wing. I fully focused on my mission, ignoring the jet behind me making its attack pass, then passing so close I could clearly hear the roar of his engines above the cockpit noises. He moved in front of me, blasting his exhaust gases straight into my aircraft, causing it to shake badly. I had to use both my feet and my hands to keep my jet straight and level, but oveflew my target. The Lighting pilot to my left signalled me again to leave, but I made a 360-degrees tun above Kyrenia, determined to complete my mission. I concluded that they did not open fire to warn me off, so they would not open fire at all: and I was flying a NATO reconnaissance jet. All the time, the Lighting on my left wing flew in formation with me. The pilot flashed the v-sign with his fingers. It was all intimidation. I opened my viewfinder, and found the target but, just as I was beginning my second photo-pass, he also broke off high, and repeated the manoeuvre, causing my aircraft to vibrate violently … at that point in time, I hit the brakes, decelerating fast, and descending to 10,000ft: they didn't expect me to do so and the Lightings overshoot well to the front. Thus, I was able to overfly my target and complete the mission: indeed, my photographs were the only successfully interpreted. While leaving Cyprus, the two RAF fighters followed me for at least 15 miles, before they broke off. I made a straight in approach to Souda.'

All the five Thunderstreaks returned safely to Souda. The engine of Papasis' jet flamed out while he was taxiing due to fuel shortage; he did not jettison empty drop tanks on the way back and they were causing additional drag and higher fuel consumption.

As most of photographs taken during his mission were too poor for interpretation, the flight at Souda received the order to launch again in the afternoon. This time, only Lieutenants Demopoulos and Papasis were underway. Once again, they were intercepted by RAF Lightnings, but this time, they completed their mission successfully.

Visible on this photograph taken in summer 1956, shortly after its delivery to the 348 Mira, is the RF-84F with US FY-serial number 53-8740; the jet piloted by Efthimios Roulias into the mission over Cyprus on 17 August 1964. (Paschalis Palavouzis Collection)

A group photo of pilots of the 348 Mira at Larissa as of May 1964, in front of the RF-84F with US FY-serial number 53-7588 – one of six jets involved in the first officially confirmed reconnaissance sortie of the RHAF over Cyprus. Visible in the centre is Colonel Constantinos A. Hatzilakos, commander of the 110th Wing. Also visible are Major Roulias (top row, fifth from the left), Lieutenant Dranias (sixth from the left), Lieutenant Demopoulos (top row, twelfth from the left), Lieutenant Papasis (top row, fifteenth from the left) and Lieutenant Papadopoulos (sixteenth from the left). Lieutenant Printzios is visible in the bottom row, tenth from the left). (Air Force Lieutenant General Konstantinos Hatzelakos Archive)

A row of RF-84Fs of the 348 Mira, as seen in 1964. This photograph nicely illustrates their general appearance, which included no fin flashes. According to unofficial Greek sources, roundels were usually applied but not worn during all of 'operational sorties over the eastern Mediterranean'. (Paschalis Palavouzis Collection)

UNARMED LIGHTNINGS

Prior to launching its intervention of 8 August 1964, Ankara notified the Headquarters of the British Forces on Cyprus that, 'offensive action would be taken against military aircraft flying on reconnaissance missions in the vicinity of Turkish naval vessels.' This mainly referred to RAF Shackleton maritime patrol aircraft tracking Turkish and Greek naval movements. The General Staff introduced this measure to ensure several hours of warning of any armed intervention so that base evacuation plans could be initiated. The British Chiefs of Staff refused to halt these flights and considered the risk to be low, as Turkish warships were not equipped with SAMs.[12]

The RAF interceptors deployed on Akrotiri as of August 1964 were Lightning F.Mk 3 of No. 111 Squadron. There was a total of nine for their annual exercise that – ironically – was planned to include lots of practice intercepts in cooperation with the British-operated radar station on the Cape Gáta. Apparently, the RAF assessed the fighter types operated by the RHAF as lacking the range to reach Cyprus, which is why the British were taken by surprise by earlier operations by Harvards and F-84Fs from the 338th Mira. The lesson was learned though and subsequently, Lightings stood quick reaction alert. The operational diary of No. 111 Squadron recorded:

> Because of this (Greek operations), the squadron placed on Lighting on 10 minutes and another at 30 minutes alert,

by day and by night. The remainder at two hours. A few scrambles were made (by day only), to identify both aircraft heading towards the S.B.A., and suspicious shipping. On 17th August, we took over the state from dawn to dusk only and the Javelins continued air night state. Before the air to ground attacks in the N.W. of the island, both RF84s and F-100s of the Turkish Air Force were identified. During the second stage when the squadron was on day alert only F-84s of the Hellenic Air Force were shadowed.

The commanding officer, Squadron Leader G. P. Black, added:

> The frequent QRA scrambles against Greek and Turkish fighters provided plenty of gossip for the crew room and bar, and at one time pilots were volunteering for the QRA roster just to get in on the act. Unlike the U.K. QRA duties however, all aircraft must remain unarmed, a fact which is kept strictly to ourselves! The health and morale of the squadron continues to remain very high.[13]

The pilot who intercepted Pritzios and forced him to jettison his drop tanks, turned out to have been Flight Officer O'Dowd. The reasons why the RAF was intercepting Greek but not Turkish aircraft, remain unknown, but were probably related to the flow of US-mediated negotiations.

Claims and Counter-Claims

As in almost everything related to Cyprus, Greek and Turkish sources are in massive disagreement regarding losses in the nine months of fighting during the First Cyprus Crisis. Total figures range between 300 and 800 killed. Although the mass of Greek reports emphasise minimal Greek Cypriot losses and next to no effectiveness of all the Turkish efforts, most reliable figures include between 133 and 174 Greek Cypriots (of which over 50 in the area between Kokkina, Mansoura and Lorovounos Mountain in August alone) and between 193 and 364 Turkish Cypriots. Between 20,000 and 25,000 Turkish Cypriots from 104 different municipalities, around 1,200 Armenian Cypriots and around 500 Greeks were displaced. At least 977 homes of Turkish Cypriots were destroyed and another 2,000 suffered severe damage and ransacking. Moreover, as up to 35 percent of the arable land in Cyprus belonged to Turkish Cypriots, the mass of whom were forced to move to enclaves covering a mere 2 percent of the total surface of the island, they were not only isolated from the rest of the country but suffered particularly severe economic damage. All the public sector workers went unpaid for almost a year, until the Turkish leadership turned the 1960 organisation into their own government, with its police, army and tax system.[14]

Field Marshall Lord Carver, who was the Deputy Commander of UNIFICYP in 1964, summed the situation up:

In Cyprus the preservation of the existing situation favoured the Turks in one respect, in that it preserved the de facto segregation arising out of the December fighting and made it appear that they could not live with the Greeks. But it probably benefitted the Greeks most, as it left them in sole charge of the Government and all its machinery, as well as control of almost all of the island.[15]

In regards of aerial operations and while the Turks claimed no Greek aircraft or helicopters as shot down, over time Greeks have claimed no less than four Turkish fighter-bombers. This figure includes one RF-84F (US FY-serial number 52-8871) supposedly shot down over Cyprus on 5 June and a T-33A the US FY-serial number of which should have ended with 4059, claimed as shot down on an unknown date. The HVKK is known to have lost one Thunderflash on 6 June, but the jet in question crashed near Finike, in Turkey, on return from a reconnaissance sortie over Cyprus and there is no evidence that it was hit by ground fire. Also written off, on 15 May 1964, was the T-33A with serial number 4050. However, the aircraft in question crashed while underway on courier duty from Ankara to Diyarbakir – which excludes the possibility of it venturing anywhere near the disputed island during its final flight. Correspondingly, the sole HVKK loss during this phase of the Cyprus Crisis was the F-100D piloted by Captain Cengiz Töpel, on 8 August 1964.

CONCLUSION

In conclusion, the Akritas Plan, as pursued by Makarios and his aides with support from Athens, failed. Principally due to its plotters underestimating Turkish Cypriot strength and resolve but also because they – and the Greek government – thought that Ankara's threat with intervention was a bluff. The fighting of 1964 thus ended without an expulsion of the Turkish Cypriot community, without its subjection to the Greek rule, and without *enosis*; indeed, without resolving any of the outstanding issues between the two communities and leaving a blazing trail of bitter hatred in its wake. The crisis thus went on and within the following years, was to bring Greece and Turkey to the brink of war at least two additional times; these stories are going to be covered in subsequent volumes of this mini-series.

DOCUMENTATION

From the British National Archives (TNA):

- The Importance to the UK of the SBAs in Cyprus (DEFE -5-189–3, 8 March 1971).
- Possible Use of Facilities in the Cyprus Base by NATO, Annex to DP.88/94, DEFE 4:173, (29 July 1964).
- *Stationing of Turkish Forces in Sovereign Base Areas in Cyprus*, DEFE 4:173, (24 July 1964).
- *Intelligence reports 1966–72*, DEFE 31:26

- WO 386/2, 'Intercommunal Fighting – Nicosia – December 1963', Joint Intelligence Group (Cyprus), Secret Intelligence Report, No. 36, 17 January 1964.
- *Chief of Staffs Committee*, DEFE 4/164, 11 February 1964.
- CAB 128/38, 'Memorandum by Prime Minister', Conclusions of a Meeting of the Cabinet, 3 January 1964.
- *Special Branch report*, CO 926/1473, March 1960
- WO386/19, Harker, D., *Notes on the Turkish Cypriot Community and Armed Forces*, 19 November 1966.

BIBLIOGRAPHY

Albrecht, G., *Weyers Flottentaschenbuch/Warships of the World, 54. Jahrgang, 1977/78* (München: Bernard & Graefe Verlag für Wehrwesen, 1978).

Adams, T, *US Army Area Handbook for Cyprus* (American University Washington, 1964)

Anderton, D, *North American F-100 Super Sabre* (Osprey, 1987)

Angelos, C. M., 'From the Creation of the National Guard to the Cypriot Army (1959–1964): The Administrative Structure and Organisation of the Cypriot Army and the Creation of Armed Groups in the two Communities', University of Cyprus, June 2013.

Anon, *Turkey and Cyprus. A Survey of the Cyprus Question with Official Statements of the Turkish Viewpoint* (Turkish Embassy, London, 1956)

Asmussen, J, *Cyprus at War: Diplomacy and Conflict during the 1974 Crisis* (Bloomsbury, 2008)

Aydin, M & Ifantis, K, *Turkish Greek Relations: The Security Dilemma in the Aegean* (Routledge, 2004)

Basara, L., *F-100 Super Sabre in Turkish Air Force, Volume 2* (Hobbytime, 2013)

Bahcheli, T, *Greek Turkish Relations Since 1955* (Westview Press, 1990)

Balchi, T, The Cyprus Crisis and the Southern Flank of NATO 1960–1975, *International Review of Turkish Studies*, Vol. 2:3, Fall 2012.

Bales, Lieutenant-General (ret.) Panagiotis, *Eagle's Orders*, (*Παρακαταθήκες Αετών*), (Athens: Infognomon Publishing, 2012)

Bernstein, B., 'The Cuban Missile Crisis: Trading the Jupiters in Turkey?', *Political Science Quarterly*, Vol. 95/No. 1, Spring 1980

Birand, M., *Shirts of Steel: An Anatomy of the Turkish Armed Forces* (I. B. Tauris: 1991)

Brown, J, *Delicately Poised Allies: Greece and Turkey* (Brassey's, 1991)

Burr, W. & Nutti, L., *The Jupiter Missiles and the Endgame of the Cuban Missile Crisis: a Matter of 'Great Secrecy'* (Wilson Center, February 2023)

Caliskan, M, *The Development of Inter-Communal Fighting in Cyprus 1948–1974* (Middle East Technical University, 2012)

Chipman, A., *NATO's Southern Allies* (London: Routledge, 1988)

Cilingir, A, *TMT: 'Ölmek var, Dönmek yok' 1957–1976* (Istanbul: Bilgeoguz, 2021)

Clark, T, *A Brief History of Cyprus* (Upper Street Press, 2020)

Clements, N, *The Battle of Kokkina* (Matador, 2018)

Coskun, O, The Cyprus Crisis of 1967 and The British-Turkish Policies (Journal of Turkish World Studies18/2, Winter 2018, pp.377–398)

Criss, N. B., 'Strategic Nuclear Missiles in Turkey: The Jupiter Affair, 1959–1963', *The Journal of Strategic Studies*, 20:30, 97–122, 24 January 2008

Daloumis, I., '112th Combat Wing' (*112 Πτέρυγα Μάχης*), *Ptisi & Diastima Magazine*, No. 132, 1996

Danisman, H., *Situation Negative: Korea 1952, An Account of Service with the Turkish Brigade* (Istanbul: Denizler Kitabevi, 2002)

Danisman, H, *Situation Negative: Korea 1952. An Account of Service with the Turkish Brigade* (Istanbul: Denizler Kitabevi, 2002)

Davies, P, *North American F-100 Super Sabre* (Crowood Press, 2003)

Denizli, A, *Kibris Baris Harekati: 20 Temmuz 1974* (Ankara, 2014)

Denktash, R, *The Cyprus Triangle*, (London: Allen & Unwin, 1982)

Dimitroulopoulos K., Brigadier-General (ret)., *In the Heights of Fighter Aircraft: Historical Documents (Στα Ύψη των Μαχητικών*

Αεροσκαφών – Ιστορικά Ντοκουμέντα), (Thessaloniki, Ydrogeios Publishing, 2007)

Dodd, C, *The History and Politics of the Cyprus Conflict* (Palgrave Macmillan, 2010)

Dodd, C, *Storm Clouds over Cyprus* (Eothen, 2002)

Dupuy, Col. T. N., Blanchard, Col. Wendell, *The Almanac of World Military Power*, (London: Arthur Barker Ltd., 1972)

Erickson, E & Uyar, M, Phase Line Attila (Marine Corps University Press, 2020)

Fanning, A., *Turkish Military in the Korean War*, (Texas Tech University, 1993)

Faroqhi, S., *Geschichte des Osmanischen Reiches* (München: C. H. Beck, 2021)

Fotakis, Z., 'Greek naval policy and the Great Powers, 1931-40', *Journal for Maritime Research*, May 2011

Francis, Brigadier H., *A Business of Some Heat: The United Nations Force on Cyprus before and during the 1974 Turkish Invasion* (Barnsley: Pen & Sword, 2004)

Gardiner, R (Ed), *Conway's All the World's Fighting Ships 1947–1982, Part 1* (Conway, 1983)

Green, W. & Fricker, J., *The Air Forces of the World* (London: MacDonald, 1958)

Göktepe, C, *British Foreign Policy Towards Turkey, 1959–1965* (London: Frank Cass, 2003)

Gurcan, M, *Opening the Black Box: The Turkish Military Before and After July 2016* (Helion, 2018)

Güvenç, S & Uyar, M, *On Contested Shores: Chapter 17: Against All Odds: Turkish Amphibious Operation in Cyprus, 20–23 July 1974* (Marine Corps University Press, 2020)

Güvenç, S & Uyar, M, *Lost in translation or transformation? The impact of American aid on the Turkish military, 1947–60* (Cold War History, Volume 22:1, 2022)

Güvenc, S & Barlas, D., 'Atatürk's Navy: Determinants of Turkish Naval Policy, 1923–1938', *Journal of Strategic Studies*, March 2003

Hale, W, *Turkish Politics and the Military* (London: Routledge, 1994)

Harker, D, *Notes on the Turkish Cypriot Community and Armed Forces* (National Archives, WO386/19, Nov. 1966)

Harlaftis, D., *My Service in the Hellenic Air Force* (*Η Πορεία μου στην Ελληνική Πολεμική Αεροπορία*), (Athens: Alexandria Publishing, 2018)

Harvey, N, *The Modern Turkish Navy and the Modern Greek Navy* (Harvey, 2016)

Hastings, M., *The Korean War: An Epic Conflict, 1950–1954* (New York: Pal Macmillan).

Henderson, N., The Birth of NATO (Weidenfeld and Nicolson, 1982)

Jenkins, G, Context and Circumstances: Turkish Military and Politics (Oxford University Press, 2002)

Joos, G., *The Canadair Sabre* (Profile Number 186), (Leatherhead: Profile Publications Ltd., 1967)

Kakolyris, I., *The Sky Warriors: Cyprus 1974, Volume A* (*Οι Πολεμιστές του Ουρανού – Κύπρος 1974, Α' Τόμος*), (Athens: privately published, 1998)

Kakolyris, I., *The Sky Warriors: Cyprus 1974, Volume B* (*Οι Πολεμιστές του Ουρανού, Οι Απέθαντοι – Κύπρος 1974 - Β' Τόμος*), (Athens: privately published, 2000)

Kakolyris, I., *The Lost Eagles Squadron* (*Η Μοίρα των Χαμένων Αετών*), (Athens: privately published, 2021)

Kandylakis, Korobilis, Daloumis, Tsonos, *Airplanes of the Hellenic Air Force, 1912–1992* (*Αεροσκάφη της Ελληνικής Πολεμικής Αεροπορίας, 1912-1992*), (IPMS Hellas, 1992)

Karatzas, A., 'SX-EAB: The Beech 18 in Hellenic Civil Aviation Agency and Cypriot National Guard' (*SX-EAB: Το Beech 18 της Υ.Π.Α και της Κυπριακής Εθνικής Φρουράς*), *IPMS Greece Magazine*, No. 40–41, 2016

Ker-Lindsay, J., *The Cyprus Problem: What everyone needs to know* (Oxford: Oxford University Press, 2011)

Keser, U., *Kıbrıs'ta Yer altı faaliyetleri ve Türk Mukavemet Teşkilatı* (Underground Activities in Cyprus and Turkish Resistance Corps) (İstanbul: IQ Yay., 2007)

Keser, U., *Kibris Türk Mücadele Tarihinde Iletisim 1954–1974* (Istanbul: Hiperlink Yayinlari, 2019)

Keser, U., *Kibris'ta, Yeralti Faaliyetleri ve TMT* (Istanbul: IQ Kültür Sanat Yayincilik, 2007)

Keser, U., *TMT'nin Görünmez Kahramanlari – Ögretmenler ve Polisler* (Ankara: Tulpars Yayinlari, 2016)

Kibaroglu, M, *Eastern Mediterranean: Countries and Issues* (Ankara: Foreign Policy Institute, 2009)

Kollopoulos, John S., 'Unwanted, Ally: Greece and the Great Powers, 1939–1941', *Balkan Studies*, 1982

Koyuncu, M & Balıkçıoğlu, E, 'The importance of organizing activities of the Turkish Cypriot Community in the process of becoming a state (1957–1960)', Journal of Human sciences, Vol. 13, Issue 3, 2016

Koumoulides, J (Editor), Cyprus in Transition 1960–1985 (London: Trigraph, 1986)

Koura, J, *Czechoslovakia and the Cyprus issue in the years 1960–1974*, Middle Eastern Studies, Volume 57, 2021, Issue 4, pp.516–533

Kuniholm, B, *The Origins of the Cold War in the Near East* (Princeton University Press, 2016)

Kyle, K., *Cyprus: In search of Peace* (Minority Rights Group Report, 1997)

Leiser, G., 'The Turkish Air Force, 1939–45: The Rise of a Minor Power', *Middle Eastern Studies*, July 1990

Lindley, D, 'Historical, Tactical, and Strategic Lessons from the Partition of Cyprus', International Studies Perspectives (2007) 8, pp.224–241

Livingston, C., 'One Thousand Wings: the United States Air Force Group and The American Mission for Aid to Turkey, 1947–50', *Middle Eastern Studies*, October 1994

Lloyd, S., *Suez 1956: A personal Account* (London: Jonathan Cape, 1978)

Mamounidakis, I, *Armour on Cyprus: Evolution and Operations* (Trojan Horse, 2008)

McDowell, E. R., *Republic F/RF-84F Thundersteak/Thunderflash in USAF - BAF - Nor AF - R Neth AF-Luft-French AF´- TAF – CNAF & RDAF Service* (Canterbury, Osprey Publications, 1970)

Mitsainas, Lieutenant-General G., *Hellenic Wings over Cyprus: First-Hand Accounts of the Operations, 1964–1974* (*Ελληνικά Φτερά στην Κύπρο: Επιχειρήσεις 1964-1974 όπως τις έζησαν και τις αφηγούνται οι πρωταγωνιστές*), (Privately published, 2011)

Murphy, C, *Modernization of the Turkish Navy* (Naval Postgraduate School, 2020)

Mütercimler, E, *Satilik Ada Kibris* (Alfa, 2007)

Necatigil, Z, *The Cyprus Question and the Turkish Position in International Law* (Oxford: Oxford University Press, 1993)

Nikolajsen, O., *Turkish Military Aircraft since 1912* (Dutch Aviation Society/Scramble, 2005)

O'Malley, B & Craig, I, *The Cyprus Conspiracy* (I.B.Tauris, 2006)

Ozer, A, *The Rise of the Turkish Defense Industry* (SETA Publications, 2019)

Pach, C., *Arming the Free World: The Origins of the US Military Assistance Programme, 1945–50* (Chapel Hill: University of North Carolina Press, 2018)

Parliament of the Hellenic Republic – Cyprus House of Representatives, *The Cyprus File, Volume A: the Findings* (in Greek), (Athens-Nicosia: official publication, 2018)

Polyviou, P, *Cyprus, Conflict and Negotiation 1960–1980* (London, Duckworth, 1980)

Provence, M., *The Last Ottoman Generation and the Making of the Modern Middle East* (Cambridge: Cambridge University Press, 2017)

Rohwer, J., Nimitz, Ch., *Seemacht: Eine Ssekgriegsgeschichte von der Antike bis zur Gegenwart* (München: Bernard & Graefe, 1974)

Sanver, A, *TMT ve Öhd Anilarim* (Lefkosa, Eylul, 2012)

Sanver, A, *Akritas'a Karsi TMT* (Lefkosa, ASralik, 2012)

Schick, I and Tonak, E, ed., *Turkey in Transition: New Perspectives* (New York, Oxford University Press, 1987)

Scutts, J., *Northrop F-5/F-20* (Modern Combat Aircraft 25), (London: Ian Allan Ltd., 1987)

Sever, M, *20 Temmuz 1974 Kibris Bitmeyen Gece* (Kastas Yayinevi, 2010)

Skeparnakos, H., *The last History Class: The Air Force through History, Junta, Attila, Troika, Powers inside Greece and Greece of the Greeks* (*Το Τελευταίο Μάθημα της Ιστορίας - – Στα μονοπάτια της Ιστορίας από μια ξενάγηση στην Πολεμική Αεροπορία – ΧΟΥΝΤΑ – ΑΤΤΙΛΑΣ και ΤΡΟΪΚΑ – Η Ελλάδα του συστήματος εξουσιών και η Ελλάδα των Ελλήνων*), (Athens: privately published, 2012)

Solesten, E. (ed.), Cyprus: a Country Study, (Washington DC: US Library of Congress, 1991)

Stafrace, Ch., *Republic F-84F Thunderstreak and RF-84F Thunderflash* (Warpaint Series No. 100), (Buckinghamshire: Warpaint Books Ltd., 2021)

Stavrinides, Z, *The Cyprus Conflict: National Identity and Statehood* (CYREP 1999)

Terniotis, Kanakaris, Markantonatos, Maglinis, *Air War over Greece (1940–1944), Vol. 1.* (*Ο Αεροπορικός Πόλεμος πάνω από την Ελλάδα (1940-1944) Πρώτος Τόμος*), (Periscopio, 2010)

Terniotis, Yiannopoulos, Maglinis, *Air War over Greece (1940–1944), Vol.2* (*Ο Αεροπορικός Πόλεμος πάνω από την Ελλάδα (1940-1944) Δεύτερος Τόμος*), (Periscopio, 2010)

Tetik, A., *North Star: Turkish Brigade in Korea* (Turkish Military History, 2007)

Thomas, N & Abbott, P, *The Korean War 1950–53* (Oxford: Osprey, 1986)

Thompson, Sir R., *War in Peace: An Analysis of Warfare since 1945*, (London: Orbis Publishing, 1981)

Türkman, S., 'Reasons for Türkiye's Intervention in Cyprus and the Cyprus Conflict 1955–64', *Turkish Military History*, No.87, 2007

Ulusoy, K, 'The Cyprus Conflict: Turkey's Strategic Dilemma', Journal of Balkan and Near Eastern Studies, 18:4, 2016

Uslu, N, *The Turkish-American Relationship between 1947 and 2003* (Nova Science, 2003)

Vlassis, S. & Paloulian, K., 'The Harvard Mission to Cyprus' (*Η Αποστολή των Harvard στην Κύπρο το 1964*), *War & History Magazine*, No. 75, June 2004

Vranas, T., '821 All-Weather Flight F-86D Sabre Dog: The last Stand' (*821 ΣΠΚ F-86D Sabre Dog: Ύστατη Προσφορά*), *Pitsi & Diastima Magazine*, No. 1, March 2006

Watson, D., *Chasing the Soft Underbelly: Turkey and the Second World War* (Warwick: Helion & Co., 2023)

Woezik, R, 'Turkish Army Aviation', *Air International*, June 1995

Yalcin, E, 'Historical Development of Cyprus and the Turkish Republic of Northern Cyprus', *International Review of Military History*, Ankara, No.87, 2007

Yellice, G., 'The American Intervention in the 1964 Cyprus Crisis, and the Greek Political Reaction (February-August 1964)', *Journal of Modern Turkish History Studies*, XVII/35, 2017

Yesilbursa, B, 'Proposals for a settlement of the Cyprus problem according to British documents 1954–1974', History Studies, Vol.11/6, December 2019

Zaloga, S, *The M47 and M48 Patton Tanks* (Oxford: Osprey, 1999)

Websites

Uknown Author, 'August 1964 – The Hellenic Air Force flies for the first time over Cyprus' (*Αύγουστος 1964: Η Ελληνική Αεροπορία πετά για πρώτη φορά πάνω από την Κύπρο*), https://defencereview.gr, 2018). URL: http://2/aygoystos-1964-i-elliniki-aeroporia-peta-gia-proti-fora-pano-apo-tin-kypro/

Uknown Author, 'Cyprus Naval Command – From its foundation to the future challenges, part A', (*Διοίκηση Ναυτικού Κύπρου: Από την συγκρότηση στις προκλήσεις του μέλλοντος -Α' Μέρος*) https://e-amyna.com/, 12/10/2017, URL: https://e-amyna.com/διοίκηση-ναυτικού-κύπρου-από-την-συγκ/

Manousogianakis S., Vice Admiral (ret.), 'The Cyprus Navy till 1974 -Formation, Coup d'etat and Turkish Invasion'(Το Κυπριακό Ναυτικό Μέχρι το 1974 – Συγκρότηση, Πραξικόπημα και Τουρκική Εισβολή), https://elinis.gr/, 08/08/2019, URL: https://elinis.gr/το-κυπριακο-ναυτικο-μεχρι-το-1974-συγκρότ/

Papadopoulos J., 'The Traumas of a Secret Mission, (Οι Πληγές μίας Μυστικής Αποστολής) https://www.kathimerini.gr, ΕΡΕΥΝΕΣ 29/04/2017, URL: https://www.kathimerini.gr/investigations/907114/oi-pliges-mias-mystikis-apostolis-stin-kypro/#webdoc

Moutsatsos D., 'The Turks burned Phaethon with napalms'- an interview to Stefanos Chelidonis, (Οι Τούρκοι έκαψαν το Φαέθων με ναπάλμ - Συνέντευξη στον Στέφανο Χελιδόνη), https://www.kathimerini.gr, 25/11/2007, URL: https://www.kathimerini.gr/society/305768/oi-toyrkoi-ekapsan-to-faethon-me-napalm/

Vogiatzis D., HAF Museum Historian, MA, PhD, 'A synopsis of the Tatoi Airfield History' (Συνοπτική Ιστορία του Αεροδρομίου του Τατοίου). (PDF) Συνοπτική ιστορία Αεροδρομίου Τατοίου | Dimitri Vogiatzis - Academia.eduhttps://www.haf.gr

Theologou A. '348 MTA – 64 years Eyes Open watchful "Eyes" of the Air Force' (348 MTA: 64 χρόνια τα άγρυπνα «Μάτια» της Πολεμικής Αεροπορίας), https://www.onalert.gr/, 03/05/2017, URL: (https://www.onalert.gr/uncategorized/348-mta-62-xronia-ta-agrypna-matia-ths-polemikis-aeroporias/128491/

Theotokatos V., Lt.General Anagnostopoulos – A patriot who stopped the Turkish Violation in the Air (Αντιπτέραρχος Αναγνωστόπουλος: Ο πατριώτης που σταματούσε τις τουρκικές παραβιάσεις), https://www.olympia.gr , 07/06/2020, URL: https://www.olympia.gr/1167183/istoria/anagnostopoulos-tourkikes-paraviaseis/

Avramidis A., 'Goodbye to a Hero of the Skies' (Αντίο σε έναν ήρωα των αιθέρων), https://www.kathimerini.gr, 2016, URL: https://www.kathimerini.gr/opinion/readers/4870384/amp-laquo-antio-amp-raquo-se-enan-iroa-ton-aitheron/

https://www.kathimerini.gr/world/870314/to-schedio-atseson-gia-to-kypriako/

NOTES

Chapter 1

1. Unless stated otherwise, this chapter is based on Provence, *The Last Ottoman Generation*; Barr, *A Line in the Sand*; Faroqhi, *Geschichte des Osmanischen Reiches*; Ker-Lindsay, *The Cyprus Problem*; Blumi, *Ottoman Refugees*; Kreiser, *Geschichte Istanbuls*; Perrett, *Desert Warfare*; Watson, *Chasing the Soft Underbelly*.

Chapter 3

1. Watson, *Chasing the Soft Underbelly*, pp.14–16.
2. Schick et all, *Turkey in Transition*, p.142.
3. Tetik, *North Star*, p.237.
4. Fanning, *Turkish Military in the Korean War*, p.81.
5. Hastings, *The Korean War*.
6. Danisman, *Situation Negative*, p.22.
7. Henderson, *The Birth of NATO*, p.105.
8. Pach, *Arming the Free World*, p.88.
9. *Ibid.*, p.208 & Göktepe, *British Foreign Policy Towards Turkey*, p.50.
10. Göktepe, *British Foreign Policy Towards Turkey*, p.8.
11. CENTO was formally dissolved in 1979 after the Iranian Revolution, although in practice it was wound down after the Cyprus conflict in 1974.
12. Birand, *Shirts of Steel*, p.195.
13. Jenkins, *Context and Circumstances*, p.15.
14. Unless stated otherwise, this and the following sub-chapters are based on Dupuy et all, *The Almanac of World Military Power*; Rohwer et all, *Seemacht*;
15. Unless stated otherwise, this sub-chapter is based on Nikolajsen, *Turkish Military Aircraft*, and Green & Fricker, *The Air Forces of the World*.

Chapter 4

1. Thompson (ed.), *War in Peace*, pp.114 & Ker-Lindsay, *Cyprus Problem*, pp.22–23.

Chapter 5

1. The National Archives (TNA), CAB 191:6, JIG (Cyprus) 1964, 27 February 1964.
2. Watson, *Chasing the Soft Underbelly*, p.72.
3. Lloyd, *Suez 1956*, p.56.
4. Burr et all, *The Jupiter Missiles and the Endgame of the Cuban Missile Crisis* & Criss, 'Strategic Nuclear Missiles in Turkey'. According to recollections of one of US Air Force officers deployed in Turkey at the time, provided in the course of an e-mail exchange in 2005 on condition of anonymity, soon after the installation of Jupiters in Turkey, the Soviet Air Force deployed a 'MiG' fighter jet in a clandestine effort to photograph the facility. The aircraft in question reached the site undisturbed and made a pass, but then crashed, killing its pilot. An inspection of the wreckage and cameras revealed that it captured very good photographs of the site, at least comparable to those taken by US aircraft over Cuba in September-October 1962. That said, and while such an effort almost certainly took place, considering the distance of Izmir from nearest air bases in Bulgaria or the USSR, it is unlikely that the aircraft in question was a MiG: fighter jets of types available at the time – like MiG-15, MiG-17, MiG-19, and MiG-21 – would have lacked the range necessary for such an operation from bases in Bulgaria or south-western USSR. Therefore, it is certain that the Soviets deployed a different type for this purpose but this was then mis-identified as a 'MiG'.
5. Dupuy et all, pp.92–93 & 117–119.

Chapter 6

1. Saka, Mehmet. *Ege Denizinde Türk Hakları*, (İstanbul: Dergâh, 1977, first published in 1955), p.65.
2. Republic of Türkiye, *Militarization of Eastern Aegean Islands Contrary to the Provisions of International Agreements* https://www.mfa.gov.tr/militarization-of-eastern-aegean-islands-contrary-tp-the-provisions-of-international-agreements.en.mfa.
3. Ergil, G, *The dark side of nationalism*, (Today's Zaman, 17 September 2008), https://web.archive.org/web/20081123064334/http://www.todayszaman.com/tz-web/yazarDetay.do?haberno=153309
4. Chrysostomou, pp.240, 248–251.
5. Unless stated otherwise, based on Ker-Lindsay, *The Cyprus Problem*; Solsten, *Cyprus: a Country Study*; Francis, *A Business of Some Heat*; Kyle, *Cyprus, in search of Peace* & Yellice, 'The American Intervention in the 1964 Cyprus Crisis'; *Special national Intelligence Estimate*, Number 29.3–64: The Cyprus Dispute, 19 June 1964 (CIA/FOIA/ERR), p.12; TNA: WO 386/2, 'Intercommunal Fighting – Nicosia – December 1963', Joint Intelligence Group (Cyprus), Secret Intelligence Report, No. 36, 17 January 1964; Chrysostomou, pp.240, 248–251; Yellice, 'The American Intervention in the 1964 Cyprus Crisis'; Ker-Lindsay, pp.34–35.
6. Notably, the first element of ELDYK arrived on Cyprus on 16 August 1960, on board the Royal Hellenic Navy's Landing Ship Tank *Limnos*. The base of the contingent was established west of Nicosia, in the Gerolakkos area, right next to the camp of the Turkish contingent.
7. *Special national Intelligence Estimate*, Number 29.3–64: The Cyprus Dispute, 19 June 1964 (CIA/FOIA/ERR), pp.12–13.
8. Yellice, 'The American Intervention in the 1964 Cyprus Crisis'.
9. Mitsainas, *Hellenic Wings over Cyprus*, pp.50.
10. *Special national Intelligence Estimate*, Number 29.3–64: The Cyprus Dispute, 19 June 1964 (CIA/FOIA/ERR), pp.12–13.
11. *Special Branch report*, CO 926/1473, March 1960.
12. Ker-Lindsay, pp.34–35 & Yellice, 'The American Intervention in the 1964 Cyprus Crisis'.
13. *Special national Intelligence Estimate*, Number 29.3–64: The Cyprus Dispute, 19 June 1964 (CIA/FOIA/ERR), p.12 & Türkman, *Reasons for Türkiye's Intervention in Cyprus and the Cyprus Conflict 1955–64*, p.287.
14. *Ibid* & Yellice, 'The American Intervention in the 1964 Cyprus Crisis'.
15. 'August 1964: The Hellenic Air Force Flies for the first time over Cyprus' (in Greek), *Defencereview.gr*, 3 November 2018.
16. TNA: OF 371/174757, 'British views on Enosis', 9 May 1964.
17. Ker-Lindsay, pp.35–36 & Yellice, 'The American Intervention in the 1964 Cyprus Crisis'.
18. TNA, *Chief of Staffs Committee*, DEFE 4/164, 11 February 1964; Ker-Lindsay, p.38. Notably, the original complement of the UNFICYP included 1,150 Canadian, 700 Finnish, 700 Swedish, 500 Irish, and 3,500 British troops led by Indian Army General Gyani.
19. TNA, 'Inward Telegram to Commonwealth Relations Office', HQ. British Forces Cyprus, 25 May 1964.
20. *Special national Intelligence Estimate*, Number 29.3–64: The Cyprus Dispute, 19 June 1964 (CIA/FOIA/ERR), p.7.
21. Vlassis et all, 'The Harvard Mission to Cyprus'.
22. The 'Parnitha' radar station was operated by the RHAF. The unit in question was established in Kavouri, outside Athens, in 1955 and initially equipped with US-made TPS-1E and TPS-10D early warning radars. In May 1958, it was re-equipped with FPS-8 sets, supported by FPS-6 height-finding radars and then established a station at Karavola, on Mount Parnitha, which resulted in its calls-sign. Notably, the unit in question remains on this site until today – of course, re-equipped with modern systems.

23. 'August 1964: The Hellenic Air Force Flies for the first time over Cyprus' (in Greek), *Defencereview.gr*, 3 November 2018.
24. Yellice, 'The American Intervention in the 1964 Cyprus Crisis'.
25. *Special national Intelligence Estimate*, Number 29.3–64: The Cyprus Dispute, 19 June 1964 (CIA/FOIA/ERR), p.13–14.
26. Nikolajsen, (former officer of the Royal Danish Armed Forces and one of leading historians of the HVKK), interview, 08/2005.

Chapter 7

1. For an analysis of communications between the enclaves see: Keser, *Kibris Türk Mücadele Tarihinde Iletisim 1954–1974*.
2. Yellice, 'The American Intervention in the 1964 Cyprus Crisis'.
3. 'Chronology June 16, 1964 – August 31, 1964', *The Middle East Journal*, Vol. 18/No. 4, Autumn 1964 & Ole Nikolajsen, interview, 08/2005 & 02/2018.
4. Mitsainas, *Hellenic Wings over Cyprus*, pp.71; 'Chronology June 16, 1964 – August 31, 1964', *The Middle East Journal*, Vol. 18/No. 4, Autumn 1964 & Ole Nikolajsen, interview, O8/2005. Notably, considering the distance from Eskisehir to Cyprus and Crete, Kalenterides' testimony is rather questionable, or there is a big problem with all of available translations of it. At least it is highly questionable if Töpel would have taken-off for a mission to attack Greek Cypriot patrol boats off the coast of Cyprus, with Souda AB as 'alternative' target. At most, it is possible that the flight plan the Greeks reported to have found in Töpel's flight suit was that for an *alternative operation*, not for an alternative target. This discrepancy was never reasonably explained by any of available Greek sources.
5. Yellice, 'The American Intervention in the 1964 Cyprus Crisis' & Nikolajsen, interview, 08/2005.
6. Mitsainas, *Hellenic Wings over Cyprus*, p.87.
7. JATO stood for 'jet-assisted take off', even though – more precisely – it was 'rocket assisted take-off'. Essentially, it consisted of attaching booster rockets under the rear fuselage to achieve a quicker take-off, especially of fully loaded aircraft on much too short runways. Once the aircraft was airborne, rockets were ejected.
8. As it turned out, the commander of the RHAF detachment forward deployed at Maritsa airfield on Rhodes was expecting a formation of RHAF T-6s (see below for details) to appear and waiting for them – instead for F-84Fs. Therefore, he was instructed to create a pretext for temporarily closing the runway of his facility, which he did, citing a failure of the runway lighting. Ironically, while forcing F-84Fs to return to Crete on last drops of fuel, this act enabled the following T-6s to proceed precisely along the plan. Moreover, the commander of the Ziros/Sitia radar station on Rhodes (operated by the 3rd Aera Control Centre), was informed that the T-6-mission was about to take place but did not expect his system to detect their low altitude approach. In order to avoid any kind of collision, he was instructed to divert any approaching aircraft away. Therefore, even if Louloudakis would have contacted the tower, he would not receive a permission to land at Maritsa.
9. Mitsainas, *Hellenic Wings over Cyprus*, p.83.
10. *Ibid.*, p.87.
11. *Ibid.*, p.89. According to Roulias' logbook two of the RF-84Fs participating on the mission were #740 and #588 (Sergios Papasis, interview with Dimitris Vassilopoulos, 01/2023).
12. TNA, *Part I to COS 50th meeting*, DEFE 4:173, (August 1964).
13. 111 Squadron Operational Record Book, August 1964.
14. Not all the displacements were long-distance. For example, about 5,000 Turkish Cypriots left the Nicosia suburb of Omorphita, for safer parts of the city.
15. Lord Carver, *Peacekeeping in Cyprus*, in J.Koumoulides, (Editor), *Cyprus in Transition 1960–1985* (London: Trigraph, 1986), p.26.

AUTHOR BIOGRAPHIES

Dimitrios Vassilopoulos was born in Athens in 1976 and works in Mechanical Engineering. From an early age he embraced aviation and went on to study aviation history. He served in the 356 Tactical Transport Squadron of the 112th Fighter Wing as a reserve sergeant, responsible for the flight line of the C-130B/H Hercules of the Hellenic Air Force, during the period 2001–2002. He also wrote a small number of articles in aviation history journals. His main field of research are the lives and actions of Hellenic parentage pilots and crews from the First World War . He has authored three books on subject, is writing the fourth and also maintains a website dedicated to the same cause, www.greeks-in-foreign-cockpits.com. This volume is his first with Helion Publishing and Tom Copper, although they have known each other for more than 20 years through the website www.acig.org.

John David Watson is an experienced public affairs professional, having written many media columns, and appeared on the TV and radio, and as military historian wrote for a number of magazines, journals, and a contributing author to several books. He is the editor of the website Balkan Military History, and is running a regular blog, Balkandave.blogspot.com. He has covered the military history of the Balkans for over 22 years, building up a large following in the social media.

Tom Cooper is an Austrian aerial warfare analyst and historian. Following a career in the worldwide transportation business – during which he established a network of contacts in the Middle East and Africa – he moved into narrow-focus analysis and writing on small, little-known air forces and conflicts, about which he has collected extensive archives. This has resulted in specialisation in such Middle Eastern air forces as of those of Egypt, Iran, Iraq and Syria, plus various African and Asian air forces. In addition to authoring and co-authoring more than 50 books – including an in-depth analysis of major Arab air forces at war with Israel in the 1955-1973 period, and over 1,000 articles, Cooper is a regular correspondent for multiple defence-related publications, and meanwhile works as editor of Helion's five @War book-series.